N2887

LEGENDS OF WARFARE
AVIATION

Vickers Wellington

The RAF's Long-Range Medium Bomber in World War II

RON MACKAY

SCHIFFER MILITARY

4880 Lower Valley Road   Atglen, PA 19310

Designed by Justin Watkinson
Type set in Impact/Minion Pro/Univers LT Std

ISBN: 978-0-7643-6529-4
Printed in China

Published by Schiffer Publishing, Ltd.
4880 Lower Valley Road
Atglen, PA 19310
Phone: (610) 593-1777; Fax: (610) 593-2002
Email: Info@schifferbooks.com
www.schifferbooks.com

For our complete selection of fine books on this and related subjects, please visit our website at www.schifferbooks.com. You may also write for a free catalog.

Schiffer Publishing's titles are available at special discounts for bulk purchases for sales promotions or premiums. Special editions, including personalized covers, corporate imprints, and excerpts, can be created in large quantities for special needs. For more information, contact the publisher.

We are always looking for people to write books on new and related subjects. If you have an idea for a book, please contact us at proposals@schifferbooks.com.

Contents

Introduction

Of the thousands of British bombers built during World War II, only a relative handful still exist in public museums or in private collections. Visitors to the Royal Air Force Museum in North London are privileged to view a comprehensive range of such designs, including one of only two examples of what ironically was produced in greater numbers (11,461) than any of its twin- or four-engine RAF contemporaries. It is the Vickers-Armstrong Wellington, affectionately dubbed the "Wimpy," the corpulent hamburger-scoffing character from the Popeye cartoons, J. Wellington Wimpy.

The twin-engine design was destined to serve in every operational theater during the century's second global conflict and did so in a variety of roles. Its initial function as a strategic bomber within the ranks of Bomber Command soon witnessed its service within Coastal Command, where it served in an antisubmarine function; it was also prominent in the art of training acolyte crews at numerous OTUs and also operated as a transport while it was utilized for test missions with experimental equipment.

It was also known as the "Cloth Bomber," thanks to the fabric that enclosed the novel geodetic structure, a framework that combined strength with flexibility. Indeed, the flexibility factor was actually visible, and it became a favorite pastime of experienced aircrew members to invite raw trainees or passengers to sit upon the main spar—and to observe their undoubtedly alarmed reaction when the central wing support spar commenced to fluctuate during engine start-up, and even more so during and after takeoff! A standard joke was centered on the aircraft's precise dimensions, in which it was claimed these were never absolutely confirmed thanks to the airframe's flexibility.

The structure was the brainchild of Dr. Barnes Wallis, the Vickers' designer, who would gain ever-lasting prominence for his creation of the "Dambuster" weapon along with the aerodynamic giants "Tallboy" (12,000 pounds) and "Grand Slam" (22,000 pounds). The geodetic principle consisted of a basket-weave system that was a crisscross pattern of self-stabilizing framework members in which loads applied in any direction were automatically neutralized by forces in the intersecting set of frames; this layout in turn provided the desired combination of high strength and low weight. The

pattern was introduced by Wallis in the construction of the single-engine Wellesley bomber, which was a private venture by the Vickers Co. K7556 took to the air in mid-1935 and was the first of 174 airframes that constituted the official Air Ministry order.

The Wellesley's success provided the spur for the company to submit plans for an all-metal, twin-engine day bomber, as laid out in the Air Ministry specification B9/32, with the geodetic principle forming the basis for the layout. The initial design centered on a high-wing, fixed-landing-gear aircraft powered by either a 660 hp Bristol Mercury VI or Rolls-Royce Goshawk steam-cooled power plant. This airframe/engine combination was regarded as more than enough to accommodate the official demand for a 1,000-pound bombload to be borne over a range of 750 miles.

However, after studying the Vickers proposal, the Air Ministry responded with a noticeably revised set of requirements in September 1933. The result was that the company design team switched their attention from a high-wing to a midwing structural layout, while the fixed landing gear was similarly displaced by retractable units. Here was the true basis for the Wellington's evolution into a much more formidable performing machine, as time would confirm. Power was to be the Goshawk 1 at this point, but as would be the case with the Spitfire, the steam-cooling system's fallibility would prove to see the engine deleted both from that fighter as well as the Wellington. In the latter instance the solution would lie with the radial-designed Bristol Pegasus, an air-cooled, nine-cylinder engine that would serve the bomber well up to the Mk. 1C; it was also the forerunner of the company's Hercules, which would supplant its cousin from the Mk. III onward.

Vickers was awarded the contract in December 1933, but at this stage it was restricted to a single prototype designated Type 271. The original fuselage layout incorporated circular Plexiglas gun-mount frames at either end; the angular-shaped cockpit framework was borrowed from the company's Stranraer flying boat. The rearward-retracting main wheels were mounted within the engine nacelles and just behind the wing spars and were enclosed in flight by front-mounted doors; finally, the fixed tailwheel was enclosed in a teardrop-pattern cover.

The sleek and overall cigar shape of prototype K4049 bears little resemblance to what would evolve as the robust and distinctly stocky outline of the production Wellington. The fixed tailwheel possesses an aerodynamic fairing, while the cockpit shape and fin/rudder structure are borrowed from the Stranraer flying boat. Landing-gear covers will be displaced by standard side-mounted doors.

The diamond-shaped geodetic design was regarded as possessing such inherent strength that the use of linear straight metal strips was kept to a minimum; for example, the prototype bore just four main strips split between the top, bottom, and sides of the fuselage; these were complemented by several supplementary strips along the fuselage sides as applied to production airframes, however. Tests carried out on the Wellesley had confirmed that comparing its geodetic layout in terms of weight/strength ratio vis-à-vis a standard square or rectangular framework elicited the following: the Vickers design weighed in at around two-thirds in comparison to its technical rival, but it conversely enjoyed an increase both in flexure and torsion strength that was virtually 100 percent.

All was ready on June 15, 1936, for the initial flight of K4049 at the hands of "Mutt" Summers, the chief test pilot. It was barely three months since he had taken the Spitfire prototype aloft, and now he was stepping into the Wellington prototype at the company's main factory of Brooklands at Weybridge, southwest of London and noted for its famous bowl-shaped car-racing track. All progressed in order with the aircraft, whose range and bombload capacity were confidently expected to match the revised 2,800-mile range and 4,000-pound statistics—a quadrupling of the original specification equivalents.

The tentative name put forward for the bomber was Crecy, a French city, and a strange choice by the Air Ministry that bucked the trend of using British city or town titles vis-à-vis multiengine aircraft. The much more appropriate Wellington title appeared within two months and coincided with the initial production order of 180. However, the Air Ministry now introduced yet another specification condition, with the aircraft being expected to conform with requirements for nocturnal operations. At the time, the act seemed contradictory, since Bomber Command was perceived as a daylight-operating entity. Indeed, apart from leaflet-dropping sorties, the emphasis during the initial months of World War II was directed toward that intention. The fact that the Luftwaffe brutally quelled any such prospects by early 1940 and accordingly forced the RAF into a night operational scenario for the ensuing four years lends a somewhat ironic twist to the request.

Among the features accommodated under such a revision was the provision of defensive armament. Although the cupolas on the prototype could accommodate single weapons, the decision was taken to fit nose, tail, and ventral turrets, with the latter being fully retractable. In addition, a flexible machine gun would be positioned beneath a sliding hatch in the central fuselage. The turrets were of Vickers origin and were hydraulically operated. Such technology was well ahead of other aviation-minded nations, including Germany, but there was a downside vis-à-vis the weapon

caliber; the .303 round in current RAF use would prove to be dangerously deficient in striking power compared to the .50-caliber bullet and, even more so, cannon-caliber equivalents. The nearest that Bomber Command attained in terms of improvement was the advent of .50-caliber machine guns equipping the FN82 and Rose Rice turrets, but neither entered service until well into 1944–45, and then only in limited numbers.

K4049 was fated not to be adapted in this defensive aspect. While under evaluation at the Aircraft and Armament Experimental Establishment, Martlesham Heath, on what was almost the last trial flight, the aircraft suddenly went out of control and into an uncontrollable high-speed dive; the pilot was fortunately cast out into midair when disintegration occurred, but his companion was not so lucky. What could have spelled deep trouble for Vickers in terms of contract restriction or even cancellation was avoided. The problem having been traced to elevator imbalance, the elevator as well as the fin/rudder structure on the B1/35 specification Warwick prototype was borrowed for attachment to its predecessor; the Wellington's future career was accordingly resurrected. (The suggestion has since been mooted that the structural alterations needed to be applied to the K4049's airframe would have proved too extensive in terms of the time needed to complete the task. Either way, their introduction on the production prototype proved perfect.)

The way ahead for the Wellington would be formidable as it and its crews undertook the launching of a strategic offensive intended to drain the life from Nazi Germany's industrial infrastructure. They would do so in the company of their Handley-Page Hampden and the Armstrong-Whitworth Whitley twin-engine contemporaries. All three designs would consciously represent the sole large-scale counteroffensive that Britain was capable of indulging within northern Europe for the ensuing two years before the full-scale appearance of four-engine successors. (A parallel land offensive had been rendered null and void following the events of May and June 1940, when its armed forces were almost peremptorily driven off the Continent, with little hope to regaining a foothold in the foreseeable future.)

The ultimately painful realization by late 1941 that the bombing offensive was virtually moribund in terms of effectiveness, while mounting in terms of losses, was very sobering, but the command would regenerate into an increasingly effective force from mid-1942 onward, under the guidance of Air Marshal Arthur "Bomber" Harris, and moreover lend its weight to the USAAF daylight offensive in an around-the-clock fashion. The Wellington, alone out of the trio of original strategic designs, would soldier on over Europe with Bomber Command until late in 1943.

A second oblique view of K4049 reveals the cockpit frame layout with its flat angular panels. The Plexiglas nose cone along with the tail cone has been covered up in order to conceal the unique geodetic internal framework from prying eyes. The landing-gear covers are more clearly outlined here. Markings are confined to six type A roundels on the fuselage and wing surfaces.

K4049 has the engines revved up to full speed, with the blades a virtually invisible blur. The nose Plexiglas affords the occupant a superb view of the aircraft's aerial surroundings but, like its future Luftwaffe contemporaries, would provide little defense against a well-directed burst of gunfire. The original mast structure behind the cockpit, which demonstrates its angular shape borrowed from the Stranraer flying boat, would be replaced by a more practical nontapered stick on production airframes.

CHAPTER 1

Construction

Fuselage

The basic framing for the fuselage consisted of a mere six transverse units. Four of these were heavy, solid units that were set up in pairs. The forward examples were positioned in the center fuselage and acted as the connecting points for the auxiliary wing spars. The second pair were more ovoid in pattern and were linked at top, bottom, and lower sides. This subsection was the linkup point for the horizontal stabilizers and vertical fin. One of the remaining pair of lighter-width units was positioned behind the cockpit to form a bulkhead. Separate geodetic panels, six in all, were jig-assembled on the center fuselage transverse frames. The side panels were continuous, whereas the top panels were separated by the cockpit space, and a similar situation applied to the two underside panels, these being separated by the bomb bay (four tubular longerons, two either side of the fuselage, acted as the pickup points for nodal points of the intersecting fuselage panels).

Wings

The equitapered wings, with an aspect ratio of 8.83, were set in a midfuselage position and were constructed on the same geodetic principle. Separate inner and outer sections linked up within the engine nacelles. The inner sections linked up to the fuselage via reinforced inner ribs. The Warren truss main spar—pin-jointed at the centerline—fed in through but was not attached to the fuselage. Fore and aft auxiliary spars were attached to the inner ribs and fuselage main frames. The auxiliary rear spar formed the support base for the split flaps and Frise ailerons. Fabric covering on the wing surfaces was completed prior to assembly with the fuselage; the latter was still left without fabric at this construction stage, in order to provide access for the bolting of the wings to the main frames.

Tail

The fin was partially geodetic in outlay and was fabric covered. Standard ribbing was applied to the upper portion, commencing almost in a line with the rudder trim-tab top edge. The main spar and the rear fin base linked up with the top of the transverse fuselage frames. The fin sloped back and had a mass balance included within the rounded top section. The rudder post formed the vertical element of the fin and possessed several hinge points for the rudder. A horn balance was mounted toward the top of the fin/rudder juncture. The rudder alone featured standard horizontal ribbing and sloped marginally forward along its length; a trim tab extended up over half the trailing edge. It, too, was fabric covered.

The stabilizer shape comprised a tapered leading edge and straight trailing edge. Two spars, the rear one forming the hinge line for the elevators, were attached to the rear pair of transverse

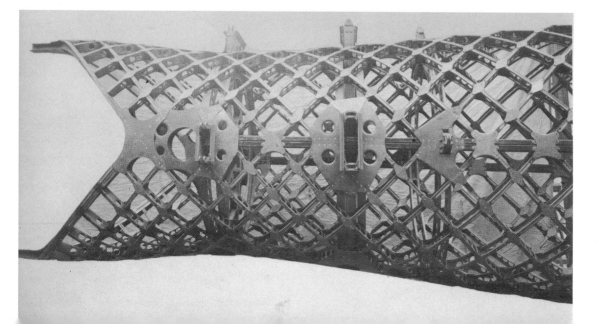

A close view of the rear fuselage frame on K4049 demonstrates the diamond pattern of the geodetic principle. Note the heavy longerons, which appear to be offset in position, with the nearside example marginally higher up the fuselage side. The two rectangular frames with lightening holes forming the stabilizer linkup to the fuselage would be replaced on production airframes. Vertical base supports for the fin and rudder are also exposed on the fuselage upper surface.

A comparison of K4049's rear structure with a standard production airframe demonstrates how the stabilizer pickup frames are absent; a horizontal triangular strip with two lightening holes, the forward edge of which lines up with the elevator-operating control ahead of the rear frame, can just be seen. The expanded depth of the fuselage is evident, as is the application of a sizable number of horizontal strips extending along its length.

fuselage frames. The elevators extended out beyond the fixed stabilizer before being curved to match up with the stabilizer leading edge. Trim tabs and horn balances were fitted, and the elevators were linked to the flaps.

Landing Gear

The main landing gear consisted of twin struts enclosing the wheel that were fitted with Vickers oleo-pneumatic shock absorbers and pneumatic brakes. They were hydraulically operated, with the Mk. I's smaller-diameter wheels being totally enclosed within the nacelle on retraction; larger-diameter substitutes on the Mk. IA forward required slots to be inserted into the door inner edges, with the lower wheel rims protruding into the slipstream in flight.

Power Plant

The twin-engine nacelles were initially equipped with the Bristol Pegasus Radial up to the Mk. IA, but several changes were then applied. The Mk. II broke the trend toward radial designs by introducing the in-line Merlin. All subsequent variants were switched back to the Bristol Hercules, apart from the Mk. IV, to which the Pratt & Whitney twin Wasp was fitted. Three-blade propellers of de Havilland, Rotol, Curtiss, or Hamilton Standard pattern were used, the sole four-blade unit being of Rotol origin that was fitted to some Mk. IIs, as well as Mks. V and VI.

Armament/Bombs

The Mk. I was equipped with nose, tail, and retractable ventral turrets possessing a total of four .303 machine guns among the trio, only the tail unit having two. The Vickers turrets gave way to Fraser-Nash equivalent turrets with doubled-up weaponry on the Mk. IA, continuing as far as the Mk. II. From the Mk. III onward, a four-gun FN20 turret supplanted the twin-gun predecessor in the tail. The ventral turret was totally dispensed with, beginning with the Mk. IC. Lateral-defense provision first appeared as a regular feature on the Mk. IC, with the original Vickers "K" weapon soon displaced by the belt-fed Browning. Ammunition caliber never advanced beyond the .303 round on the Wellington.

The longitudinal beams built into the bomb bay strengthened the airframe at the expense of lateral space. The result was that standard bombs above the 250-pound weight, other than the slimline 1,000-pound armor-piercing (AP) bomb or the 18-inch torpedo, could not be regularly borne without modifying the structure. The Type 423–prefixed modification was carried out in limited numbers, so that the Wellington could accommodate the 4,000-pound "Cookie."

Crew

The crew provision of six included two pilots, the other four positions covering the navigator, wireless operator, and two air gunners. As the need for aircrew numbers began to be overtaken by the ever-expanding bomber offensive, the decision was taken for the second pilot position to be phased out. This requirement assumed more justification, given the reverse decision to split the duties of the observer (who was performing the joint functions of navigator and bomb aimer when World War II commenced) into separate aircrew grades.

Here are the four types of transverse fuselage frames. On the right are the two more-solid units to which the wing spars are attached; next to them is the cockpit bulkhead, with the vertical strut in the center. The conjoined pair of frames with the V pattern on the lower sides composes the stabilizer securing units, while the farthest left frame is inserted in the central fuselage.

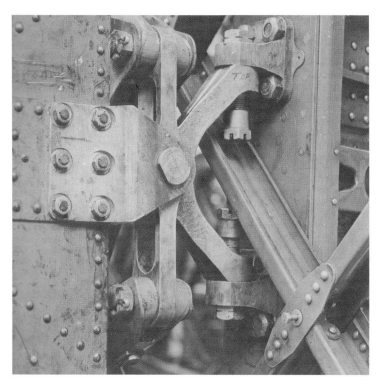

The Mk. I airframe seen under construction is believed to be the first production example, L4212. This is apparently the case, to judge by the short-length window section on the forward fuselage directly behind the cockpit frame. Subsequent airframes featured an extended version reaching back to just beyond the wing trailing edge.

The main spar floats freely through the fuselage, the connecting loads between wings and fuselage being transferred by front and rear spars via heavy root ribs bolted to the two central transverse frames positioned over the center and rear of the bomb bay. Seen here is the forward spar attachment.

The adaptation of the Warwick's fin/rudder and stabilizers to the production airframe L4212 was not the sole (albeit the most crucial) alteration arising from the loss of K4049. The borrowing of the Stranraer cockpit frame for the prototype also cast up a negative reflection effect upon the pilot's vision due to the angular flat panels encompassed therein, according to those carrying out test flights. The result was the introduction of side panels contoured to the fuselage cross section, along with flat panels for the windscreen. The effect when testing L4202 was as anticipated; namely, the cutting down of sun glare and reflection experienced with K4049. A third adaptation was the removal of the spat cover on the tailwheel and the unit's conversion from a fixed to a retractable status.

The anticipated linking of the Pegasus XVIII to L4202 was not achieved at the stage of flight testing, due to production tests still being in progress, so the aircraft went aloft with Pegasus XX alternatives on December 23, 1937. The nose and tail platforms were now fitted with the Vickers gun turrets, incorporating Nash and Thompson controls. In practice, they were to prove fatally deficient in gun traverse and, in the case of the former unit, totally inadequate in firepower since the gunner operated just one machine gun. The debate on whether they should be replaced was to be hotly disputed by the company, but a change would be brought to bear with the Mk. 1A, albeit not before several initial battles with the Luftwaffe would sadly cast up their almost total failure as a viable defensive source.

A continuing tendency for nose-heaviness, although not so severe as that experienced on K4049, was finally countered, first by fitting horn balances on production airframes from L4013 onward. A reverse tendency toward tail-heaviness was similarly

L4212 is seen following completion and removal from the production line. The nose turret, which is a Vickers product, reveals the narrow slit through which the .303 gun barrel protruded; the degree of lateral movement was seriously limited in effect compared to the later replacement Frazer Nash turret, which enjoyed superior vertical and azimuth traverse.

The second production prototype, L4213, is seen minus the propeller spinner fairings that became standard on Pegasus-powered Wellingtons. The distinctive bar link mounted between the wheel hubs and support struts is also on view. This bomber never witnessed operational service and was finally relegated to ground instruction duties during December 1940.

An early production Mk. I Wellington has been caught on camera while gently banking to starboard over the river Wey as it commences its landing approach to Vickers-Armstrong's Weybridge airfield in 1938. The small shape seen under the forward fuselage is the venturi for the pilot's blind-flying panel, almost a standard item on Wellington variants up to the Mk. IC.

A second picture of L4212 catches the production prototype as it is being moved, albeit not under its own power. The stretch of water forded by the bridge, over which personnel are manhandling the Mk. I "Wimpy," is a section of the river Wey. The aircraft never flew on operations but instead served in an experimental role with the Aircraft and Armaments Experimental Establishment (AAEE) and the Royal Aircraft Establishment (RAE).

tackled successfully by linking the operation of the flaps with the elevator trim tabs. Provision for cockpit heating and deicing equipment to counter ice accretion was made, especially given that future operations were anticipated to be conducted at anything up to around 15,000 feet. Finally, the introduction of de Havilland / Hamilton three-blade, constant-speed propellers on the aircraft boosted its climb rate and sustained altitude capability. Defensive firepower apart, the Wellington was bidding fair to become an important element in Bomber Command's striking force—a supposition that was becoming more and more clear as Europe lurched toward its second Armageddon within the first half of the twentieth century.

Production was slow to gain pace, with the main Vickers plant initially pushed to complete one airframe per day during the approximately fourteen-month spell beginning in July 1938, which involved 181 Mk. Is; a second, mixed batch of twenty Mks. I and IA would be turned out between August 1939 and April 1940. The first Mk. I to reach squadron service arrived at Mildenhall (No. 99 Squadron) in October 1938, and a steady flow of the variant had joined seven more units, all based with No. 3 Group in East Anglia prior to the declaration of war. A further two squadrons, Nos. 75 and 148, stationed at Harwell with their Mk. I complement, were placed on group reserve status.

Weighing in at an all-up-weight (AUW) figure of 24,850 pounds, the Mk. I's performance figures were assessed as follows. Maximum speed was worked out at 245 mph, range was calculated at a maximum figure of 2,200 miles, and maximum ceiling was figured at 21,600 feet. The bombload was advanced in terms of the 1930s, being 4,500 pounds. In practice, the carriage of a full load would tend to limit the range to well below the maximum figure, while maximum altitude would be similarly inhibited in this operational respect.

A lineup of Mk. Is have been snapped sometime during 1938, ready for delivery to the RAF. L4226 (*left*) was in succession assigned to No. 99 Squadron, followed by service with No. 20 Operational Training Unit (OTU); L4296 (*center*) was dispatched to No. 38 Squadron.

Vertical-angle shot of two Mk. I Wellingtons flying in close formation during the same air defense exercise shows how the white crosses almost obliterate the type B roundels. The fabric covering to the wing surfaces cast up a dappling effect as they flex under the influence of the airflow. Note the separate scheme "A" and "B" camouflage patterns, with the A scheme flowing to the left on the right-hand bomber and in reverse style on the other aircraft.

A duo of No. 39 Squadron Mk. Is squatting on the grass surface of Marham in Norfolk are immersed in the gloom of a typical British weather scenario. NH: R displays the typical large code letters prevalent during the late 1930s, along with a type A fuselage roundel.

Mk. I L4341 has white crosses applied to the center of the fuselage and wing roundels; these denote the No. 214 Squadron aircraft as a Westland machine performing in an air defense exercise launched during August 1939. The camouflage pattern is the "B" scheme, which extends forward from port to starboard; the "A" pattern is applied in the reverse direction.

World War II had barely commenced when this picture of No. 9 Squadron Mk. Is flying in a somewhat loose formation was taken. The distinctive Vickers nose turret, twin radio masts, and unfaired D/F loop were regular features on the Mk. I. The squadron badge on the nose bears a motto in Latin that translates as "Throughout the night we fly"—but the crews' interpretation was more blunt and heartfelt: "There is always 'bloody' something!!"

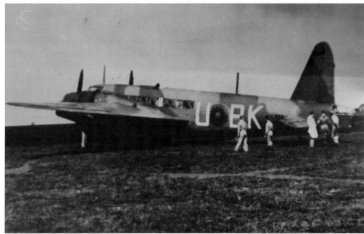

Bomber Command squadron code letters underwent several changes on either side of World War II's launch. In this case, the BK letters seen on this Mk. I denote No. 115 Squadron around the time of the 1938 Munich Crisis. The dulling-down of the roundel's light central color was intended to mask the bomber from being picked up by the opposition, whether fighters or searchlight batteries were concerned. L4221 ended up with a general reconnaissance unit until late 1941.

L4273 was a Mk. 1 from the original production batch of 175. The permanent hangar outside which she is parked indicates her original assignment to No. 9 Squadron, then stationed at Honington, Suffolk. The bomber survived operations and service with two OTUs before becoming a ground instructional machine starting in November 1942. The large underwing serial was intended as an antidote against low-flying activities.

During April 1940 a Mk. I Wellington from No. 215 Squadron was dispatched to Wick in northern Scotland. The sortie, comprising a 2,000-mile round-trip flight, was intended to monitor Kriegsmarine dispositions around Narvik in northern Norway, a Royal Navy observer being included for this purpose. A group of Mk. I Hurricanes are seen in the foreground as the bomber clears the airfield perimeter.

A crew member on the Narvik-bound "Wimpy" is attending to the flare chute. Immediately behind him is the ventral turret, while the circular shape on the port side is arguably more important—the Elsan chemical toilet! The semicircular pads on the window frames were used as headrests by the crew when carrying out prolonged observation. The rest bunk is seen in the right foreground.

The prominent structure of the Eiffel Tower in the center of Paris, France, is being overflown by two Mk. Is; the nearside bomber carries the code letters for No. 149 Squadron, whose letters would change to OJ by the end of 1939. The occasion of this courtesy visit was the celebration of Bastille Day on July 14.

The wing-mounted fuel tanks were assembled as a single overall unit, but with the twin rows of three tanks straddling the main spar. Note how the tanks are tapered in an outward direction to conform with the equitapered wing layout. When in place, longitudinal straps on each tank surface act as supports. Incredibly, the Mk. I tanks were bereft of any self-sealing facility, an indefensible situation resolved only during the 1939–40 winter.

Production is in full swing in this picture, with at least twelve fuselage sections on display. Most lack the nose platform on which the Vickers gun turret will rest. The tensile and torsion strength of the seemingly frail geodetic structure was around double that of a standard square or rectangular equivalent.

A closer view of the nearside pair of Mk. I fuselages within what is probably the same lineup provides a good view of the overall geodetic-based structure. Note the cockpit bulkhead, which is formed by one of the two light transverse frames. The nose plinths have now been attached and reveal the opaque lower sides of the Vickers nose turret, with its narrow access for the single machine gun.

Assembly workers are busy applying the fabric covering to a Mk. I's geodetic skeleton. The engine baffle plates have nine eyelet apertures through which cooling air is directed onto the cylinders; the pattern was seen on the Pegasus engines, which powered the "Wimpy" up to the Mk. 1C.

The seemingly pastoral surroundings within which a pair of Mk. Is are seen parked are hardly reminiscent of a nation on the brink of prosecuting a conflict, or even the indication of an active RAF airfield. Each squadron possessed a satellite airfield that was basic in layout, a fact that could explain the surroundings seen here. Although blurred in quality, the BS unit letters can be discerned; however, none of the No. 3 Wellington group squadrons were allocated the letters.

Three Vickers Co. pilots are trekking out toward a line of Wellingtons, which in the case of the examples on either fringe are reportedly serving with No. 38 Squadron. All three are likely present at Weybridge due to their requiring major repair or were brought here for modification. Picture was taken immediately prior to or soon after hostilities commenced.

This picture is recorded as being taken during the initial months of World War II, with the six-man crew fully kitted up in Sidcot suits and wearing their parachute harnesses. The photo detail of the Wellington does not allow confirmation of whether it is a Mk. I or Mk. IA. The confident expectations regarding completing a sortie in absolute security from loss were to be shattered by December 1939.

In the several-month spell preceding the outbreak of hostilities, No. 3 Group, in common with the other heavy elements of Bomber Command, had seen its flying-training program granting top priority to close-formation activity; this aspect of future operations was predicated on the swiftly disabused theory that the defensive armament would prove more than sufficient to ward off enemy fighter assault and even inflict as much if not more casualties among the opposition. (History now reveals the naive thinking behind the plan's confident stance. However, the RAF authorities had no practical experience to act in a manner that might have avoided the looming cataclysm that engulfed first No. 3 Group and later the Battles and Blenheims of No. 2 Group, as they in turn were crucified during the Battle of France.)

Mk. IA

The immediate successor to the Mk. I incorporated several improvements in technical content as well as reflecting features that were already in the pipeline for the Mk. II. The AUW figure was assessed at 28,000 pounds, a factor that called for a strengthened landing gear possessing larger wheels; the hitherto entire enclosure of the wheels within the nacelle was no longer possible, so slots were cut out of the door edges, through which the lower wheel rims protruded when in flight. In addition, the center of gravity (C of G) was moved marginally forward to counter these adjustments. An astrodome was introduced several feet behind the now-faired-in D/F loop, the former-named item introduced with the navigator's need to use his sextant—a necessary act in view of the current lack of electronic assistance for this vital member of any bomber crew. A second necessary addition was the fitting of fuel-jettison pipes. The installed bomb gear and oxygen equipment were specific items also envisaged for the Mk. II. The overall performance was roughly akin to the Mk. I, even allowing for the AUW increase.

One peculiarity involving the Pegasus engines was the difference in exhaust pipe length between each duo when in position. Whereas the portside pipe extended to just beyond the wing leading edge, its companion was foreshortened in length to finish just behind the cowling end. The problem arose during engine start, when flame streaking sometimes occurred, an act that could easily set the underwing fabric on fire. The risk was countered in an ad hoc manner by a ground crew member holding a bucket over the pipe orifice! The technical solution was to be the fitting of a barbed flame damper (the port exhaust pipe was modified with a circular muff fitting in the center that served as part of the fuselage-heating system).

The debate about adequate defensive armament that had so aroused opposition to any change from Vickers was settled in

An oblique-angle picture of a Mk. 1A Wellington demonstrates a degree of aerodynamic cleanup; this takes the form of a cover to the D/F loop and the deletion of the rear radio mast. The substitution of the original Vickers gun turrets with the more efficiently functioning Frazer Nash units can be seen in the case of the forward example, which moreover increased the firepower from one to two .303 machine guns.

favor of the Frazer Nash Co.'s FN5 and FN10 hydraulically operated turrets, both possessing twin .303 machine guns, which were superior in elevation and azimuth respects. Ventral cover was to be provided by an FN9 unit mounted directly behind the bomb bay, in similar fashion to the Mk. I. In practice the fitting was subsequently deleted on the Mk. IA, a major limiting factor occurring with its lowering in flight that naturally reduced forward speed, while an inability to carry out an overall scan of the sky probably strengthened the case for withdrawal. Laterally positioned defensive cover, such as, for example, the B-17 and B-24, was absent at the time, an omission that would add to the Wellington crews' travails during the first months of World War II, especially given the intention for Bomber Command to operate by day

Production of the Mk. IA was almost wholly concentrated on the Weybridge factory, but plans were by now well advanced for the first of two "Shadow" plants to be created. The first of these was located at Chester (Broughton), which, although originally a 1936 company-planned and company-owned site, was taken over by the government in 1938 and was functioning in time to catch the very tail end of Mk. IA production by turning out seventeen of the overall batch of 183. Delivery to operational squadrons commenced on the very eve of Britain's September 3 declaration of war, with N2865-67, the airframes concerned, being delivered to No. 149 Squadron.

Unlike Weybridge, where Wellingtons were assembled on site from start to finish, both Broughton and subsequently Blackpool

A lateral view of the same Mk. IA Wellington shows up the relatively clean outline of the airframe. The photo angle picks out the much-needed improvement in defensive firepower compared to the Vickers-armed Mk. I, with FN5 and FN10 twin-gun turrets in the respective nose and rear locations. Note the air scoop directly behind the bomb bay. Markings are restricted to fuselage and upper-wing roundels.

(Squires Gate), where assembly commenced during 1940, were intended to act as mass-production assembly plants, with the components being delivered from outside sources. By the time production had totally ceased in late 1945, the two mass assembly plants had completed 78 percent (8,946) out of the overall figure of 11,461 Wellingtons.

The distribution of production to locations other than the various main company factories was as much a defensive measure against likely crippling assault as it was an intention to spread the load of overall production across the national landscape. In the case of Weybridge, this plan paid unconscious dividends during the Battle of Britain, albeit in a manner immediately deleterious to Wellington production. On September 4, Erprobungsgruppe 210's Bf 110s, dispatched to assault the Hawker factory at the other side of the airfield from Vickers, mistakenly released their bombs upon the latter structure, causing instant dislocation to the assembly lines and heavy staff casualties. Lord Beaverbrook, minister for aircraft production, ordered manufacturing to be suspended at Weybridge and concentrated at alternative sources, with the main plant concentrating on final assembly; it would be the following early spring before Weybridge would resume complete Wellington airframe production.

Operational Realities

The stated intention for Bomber Command to conduct active operations over Germany was to remain moribund up to the late spring of 1940. As a virtually fruitless and soon brutally rebuffed alternative, the Wellington and its companion designs would fly "armed reconnaissance" sorties over the North Sea that fell short of any land-directed assaults other than attacking shipping, laying off any seaport or naval base. The first such raid was launched on September 4 and included fourteen Wellingtons out of the twenty-nine-strong force. The attempt to attack naval units off the northwestern German coast ended with little success; five Blenheims, and Mk. Is L4268 and L 4273 of No. 9 Squadron, were posted missing in action.

The bomber crews subsequently limited their sorties to the midpoint of the North Sea up to December 1939, but the minimal number of individual sorties flown would have presented no disruption to Kriegsmarine or commercial shipping traffic. Matters took a turn during the final month, but wholly for the worse within the command's ranks. The first raid encountered fighter opposition but no losses among the Wellington force, while seaplane-base patrols were similarly free of opposition. Then came the fourteenth and the initial exposure of the Vickers bombers to their manifold weaknesses. No. 99 Squadron headed out to shipping roads off Wilhelmshaven and returned several hours later with five out of the twelve aircraft dispatched, victims of a combined fighter/flak counterforce.

Four days later, any doubts regarding an ability to stave off the defenders with minimal losses were even more tragically exposed. The extended period during which the twenty-two crews from the three-squadron formation flew in toward and then down along the coastal area prior to heading home provided more than ample time for the German radar system to direct a mix of Bf 109s and Bf 110s that latched onto their adversaries in the clear skies. The Jagdwaffe pilots experienced little problem in striking home with virtual impunity against even the better-armed Mk. IAs on hand, five of whom from No. 9 Squadron were among the ultimate loss tally. The striking power of the .303 bullet was greatly inferior, even assuming the fighter closed to within range.

Adding to the carnage was the unbelievable lack of self-sealing capability on the fuel tanks, an almost criminal technical lapse; even when not erupting in fire when the surfaces were penetrated, the subsequent accelerated draining of the content almost certainly ensured the affected bomber's loss through a shortage of reserves and descent into the sea. A third operational disability likely arose from the lack of lateral armament; the Bf 110 pilots could fly parallel to a Wellington and the rear gunners engage the target with no real chance of a response from their turret gunner adversaries. The one-sided air battle concluded with fully twelve crews MIA, and any residual prospects for the self-defending-formation concept to prove effective had been torn to shreds. Here was the catalyst for RAF daylight strategic operations to be indefinitely suspended—a bitter lesson that would hold sway for the ensuing period of the conflict up to around D-day.

Operational Pros and Cons

The switch to nocturnal operations occurred with the Nazi onslaught in the West. A major limitation in carrying out the bombing offensive, one that was not really exposed until the Butt Report in late 1941, was the ability of the crews to attain their briefed targets. Electronic navigational equipment did not exist as World War II progressed through its initial stages. All a navigator possessed in this respect was a sextant with which to "shoot the stars"—all right if clouds did not intervene. Otherwise he had to work on deducing an accurate course by using visual references to back the briefed wind speeds. It was difficult enough to track

down a major source such as an individual town or city; with almost unbelievable naivety, the "powers that be" not only allotted specific targets to the crews but dispatched them in single manner; the latter action proved increasingly lethal as the *Nachtjagd* (Luftwaffe night fighters) was steadily built up in response to the RAF threat and would be at least only partially countered by the creation of the "bomber stream" concept from mid-1942 on.

The extended passage over the North Sea held the constant danger of ditching should the bomber be fatally crippled or run out of fuel. To counter the risk of the aircraft sinking too quickly for the crew to get out into their dinghy, flotation bags were mounted in the upper bomb bay. These were naturally to be inflated prior to striking the water, but an even more mandatory requirement was for the bomb bay doors to be closed. The bracing of the bags against the door surfaces was expected to provide the basic resistance intended to absorb the tremendous force of impact with the water. A subsequent survey of Wellington ditching confirmed the validity of the fitting, since 101 of the 124 individuals manning the twenty aircraft lost came through the experience alive, a figure well ahead of the Wellington's Bomber Command contemporaries.

The disaster of the December 18 Heligoland air battle with the Luftwaffe is just seventy-two hours distant from this picture taken at Mildenhall, destined to be a long-term home for No. 149 Squadron; three of its Mk. IAs are arrayed in the background. Whether any of the crew members seen here were involved in the action, the bald fact is that the majority among their number would be fortunate to survive their operational tours, such would be the horrendous scale of loss among Bomber Command personnel across the ensuing five years.

The crash-landed state of this Mk. 1A attests to this rueful but honest remark among RAF aircrew: "A good landing is one you walk away from!" In this case, the bomber is serving at No. 20 OTU, located at Lossiemouth in northeastern Scotland. The collapsed main wheel and twisted propeller blades indicate the incident occurred during the landing.

A trio of Mk. 1A Wellingtons are holding a neat "Vic" formation as they overfly their airfield at Bassingbourn (later home for the 91st Bomb Group) during the summer of 1940. The bombers now serve with No. 11 OTU but are still retaining their former LG codes for their time with No. 215 Squadron. The underwing type A roundels are destined to be deleted from Bomber Command aircraft during World War II's course.

A ground view of the same trio, with LG: G in the center, reveals how the camouflage separation line is still running along the lower line of the fuselage. This contrasts with the aircraft (*right*), where the black underside color is raised higher up the fuselage at a point behind the wing trailing edges. The Mk. 1A generally lacked the Lorenz blind-landing rod beneath the rear fuselage, its wholesale introduction occurring only with the Mk. 1C's arrival.

A publicity picture of a Mk. 1A that is bereft of its defensive armament unconsciously confirms how vulnerable the RAF bombers were to aerial assault from this ventral angle. The deletion of the original underside turret on the "Wimpy" would prove costly as the Nachtjagd Bf 110s and Ju 88s built up in sizable numbers from 1940–41 on.

Yet another Wellington has come to an untidy conclusion during either its takeoff or landing attempt. The absence of squadron codes suggests the aircraft is relegated from frontline operations and assigned to a training unit. The seeming absence of a Lorenz blind-landing rod under the rear fuselage indicates the aircraft is a Mk. 1A.

The bomb-spitting-devil artwork and the cheery expressions on the four airmen serving as ground crew cannot conceal the bald fact that Bomber Command's bombs—a 250-pound example of which is on the trolley—were, by 1940–41, having at best an extremely minimal effect on German industry. Note the cutback in the nose section, permitting the gun turret to fully traverse. Photo believed taken at Feltwell, home for No. 75 (New Zealand) Squadron.

A six-man crew, all of whom are sporting sleeveless flight jackets, are standing rather close to the port engine on Mk. 1A N2912, which is being revved up to a full pitch. The permanent hangars confirm that Bassingbourn is a prewar planned airfield. This No. 11 OTU Wellington was the victim of a I./NJG 2 Ju 88C on April 24, 1941, when it crashed onto a fellow bomber, R1404; two of the crew were killed.

RAF aircraft that survived their operational "tours" and were deemed ready for retirement from frontline duties were regularly assigned to OTUs or similar second-echelon units. The somewhat weatherworn condition of N2887, at least on her upper surfaces—the pristine black areas a recently applied contrast—attests to her time with No. 99 Squadron as LN: J. Now she is bringing trainee crews up to operational readiness at one of the six support units she served with up to April 1945, when she was "struck off charge" and scrapped.

The nocturnal operational atmosphere is caught here as the six-man crew of a Wellington are in the process of entering their mount via the underside hatch in the nose of a Mk. 1A or C. The picture can be roughly dated to the 1939–42 period of operations, when the sixth member was the second pilot. This position was deleted from "Wimpy" crew complements for the remainder of World War II onward.

The bleak winter weather experienced during 1940–41 probably matches Britain's military fortunes at this time. The camera is focused on what appears to be a Mk. 1A, since it lacks a Lorenz blind-flying rod. Aircraft belongs to No. 311 (Czechoslovakian) Squadron, operating out of East Wretham. The unit's practice of painting out the white in the fuselage roundel is rather compromised by retention of the thick yellow outline.

A wealth of detail is visible on a Coastal Command Mk. 1A that is being stripped down by a group of WAAFs. The port outer wing is detached, and the innards of the Pegasus engine are revealed along with the exhaust pipe, which bears a heating-muff attachment. The unit codes are believed to be HR but cannot be traced to a specific unit, although some sources suggest a link with No. 304 (Polish) Squadron.

Inflatable bags attached to the roof of the bomb bay were intended to assist a crew in achieving a successful impact with the sea when ditching that would leave the airframe intact. The bags would make direct contact with the closed bomb bay doors to present the necessary counterforce against the deceptively smooth but practically unyielding nature of water.

The total lack of defense against laterally delivered Luftwaffe fighter assault was addressed only during the winter of 1939–40. The single .303 Vickers gas-operated (VGO) "K" machine gun, with a hundred-round ammunition pan on top, is slotted into a gap in the Plexiglas, now bearing a metal surround riveted in place. Also evident are the screws and one of the several vertical strips securing the overall window frame in position on the fuselage. The Vickers weapon would swiftly be replaced by a .303 Browning belt-fed equivalent.

Although the duty of carrying out leaflet-dropping operations during 1939–40 was allocated to the Whitleys of No. 4 Group, there was a degree of support from other groups. This burned-out airframe of a Mk. I Wellington under German inspection follows the bomber's loss during such a sortie known as "Nikelling" conducted early in 1940.

CHAPTER 3
DWI

The distinctive shape of a directional wireless installation (DWI) Wellington is seen from an aerial vertical angle. The first four airframes converted to the mine-destruction duty were P2511, 2518, 2521, and 2522.

Between the declaration of war and the end of 1939, the Germans commenced the laying of magnetic mines in the shipping lanes lining the coasts of southern England, with the North Sea a leading target. The weapons were anchored to the sea base and were detonated by the reaction of vessel hulls when they steamed over each specific location. The result was an alarmingly expanding casualty rate among both naval and commercial traffic, to which there was no immediate countermeasure. The bid was an element of the grand plan to blockade the British Isles and thereby cause the government to surrender due to the ultimate dearth of food and other material supplies with which to sustain the conflict.

The discovery of a mine that had been washed ashore revealed the weapon's function, whereupon a passive means of neutralizing its malign effect was brought into use. This consisted of degaussing gear (Professor Gauss, the inventor, ironically being of German origin), which nullified the magnetic influence of the hull in being attracted to by the mine. A more active method was introduced in the form of an aircraft-based device that reversed the procedure by creating a magnetic field that induced the mine's attraction and consequently its detonation.

The Vickers Co. was directed to modify several Wellingtons to carry the necessary equipment, which consisted of a generator with which to create and sustain an electromagnetic field. The field in turn was generated by an aluminum coil initially enclosed within a thin, 51-foot-diameter balsawood frame. The several subframes were assembled prior to being slung underneath the aircraft and attached at four points to the nose, rear ventral fuselage, and wings; the effect was a slightly angled-up appearance when viewed from a lateral angle.

Any apprehension concerning adverse aerodynamic effect upon the aircraft's flight performance proved unfounded after a frame was fitted to a Mk. IA (P2518), and subsequent flight tests were conducted with the aluminum strip coil inserted. The gun turrets had been detached and cone-pattern fairings took their place on this and all subsequent airframes, although later examples bore clear-piece equivalents in the tail. In addition, all nonessential equipment was taken out of the fuselage interior. Vickers modified four more airframes, but a combination of production and experimental priorities witnessed a further eleven modifications carried out at Croydon, with the Rollason Co. carrying out the airframe adaptation along with English Electric, whose staff produced the coils.

The coils were initially powered by Ford V-8 engines driving 35 kw Maudsley generators. The lighter but more powerful Gypsy Six motor, which drove a 95 kw generator delivering an enhanced magnetic field, as well as being 1,000 pounds lighter, was subsequently installed within what was termed the DWI Mk. II. The rings were also reduced to 48 feet on the eleven DWI Mk. II aircraft that furthermore were adapted from Mk. I stock. An ironic physical condition arose during the tests. Despite what was the consistently coldest winter in years, the heat generated by the equipment raised temperatures to over triple-digit degrees, akin more to equatorial conditions. The result was that the crew were often reduced to minimal clothing levels, including working minus their shirts! The provision of air ducts did at least alleviate the situation but never provided a perfect answer. A duct system similarly cooled the coil frame interior.

An anonymous DWI Wellington is surrounded by the huge circular balsa casing housing the aluminum coil, which is ready for attachment to the fuselage. The flight characteristics of the bomber were not adversely affected by the extra aerofoil, although careful use of the trim mechanism in the cockpit was indulged.

The initial tests were conducted overland, with the airfield at Boscombe Down the chosen location. A defused mine duly provided the target, which elicited a positive reaction from the airborne set. However, there were several factors that had to be considered before practical in-the-field results could be expected to occur. The first was the question of the mine's depth under the water, which would determine the degree of the magnetic field directed at the weapon that was required to achieve detonation.

Then the altitude at which to fly in order to effect a positive outcome was another critical issue, and one that could easily put aircraft and crew at risk should the detonation be heavy enough to respectively inflict serious or even fatal damage or injuries or fatalities. The original estimated height for the equipment to succeed was set at 60 feet. (Bear in mind the reaction of W/Comm. Guy Gibson when presented with this need for the "Dambusters" raid: "You have only to hiccup and you are in the 'drink' [water].") Imagine the DWI pilots' reaction, then, when the altitude was further reduced to 35 feet. Now, the risk of being caught in the water plume cast up by the mine's explosion was matched by the equal risk of making inadvertent contact with the sea; such was the very slim margin between security and catastrophe should the pilot make a misjudgment.

The third critical factor involved the speed at which the search could be conducted, as well as the angle of the coil circle in order to achieve maximum effect. The speed had to be slow enough in order to ensure that the magnetic field not peak for too short a period of time to trigger off the weapon; conversely, the pace should be such that the aircraft was not damaged by the detonation. The angle of the coil frame being tilted upward in relation to the Wellington required a nose-down-trim flight attitude for the frame to align parallel to the sea surface. That was all there was to it.

Whereas the "Dambuster" crews were tasked with the single sortie flown, the manifold risks to a successful DWI sweep were to be faced on every occasion. The first active duties were flown from Manston, Kent, in southeastern England by the crews assigned to No. 1 General Reconnaissance Unit (GRU). The first recorded success was on January 8, 1940, followed by a second five days later. Disaster was narrowly avoided on the latter occasion when the extreme proximity of the detonation to the bomber blew the hatches off, with the accelerometer recording 10 g. However, a postoperation examination of the airframe by Vickers staff disclosed no structural damage, thus once again confirming the tremendous integrity of the geodetic system.

The standard P4 compasses were thought to be inoperable due to the presence of the DWI equipment, and so recourse was had to the air-driven gyro direction indicator (GDI). This gear had to be set up by utilizing a stretch of straight railroad line near No. 1 GRU's airfield. A subsequent test of the P4 compass by mounting it in the rear fuselage, where it was free from structural influence, proved its ability to function fully, and so the fallible GDI was dispensed with. A further adaptation to the DWI system was the installation of a two-way directional operating switch. This permitted a reversal of the magnetic coil's influence from the normal north-seeking thrust to a south-seeking direction, in order to activate mines whose polarization had been so set.

The duo of trial aircraft (P2518 and 2521) had carried out the original sweeps but were soon supplemented by the first Gypsy Six–equipped Mk. IIs, L4356. Plans were duly put in force for all three to conduct combined "sweeps" with a view to increasing the overall magnetic field. The rate of success was steady rather than spectacular, but the presence of up to six DWI Mk. II aircraft proved a definite advantage. By April, a second GRU unit was created and based farther north at Bircham Newton, Norfolk.

The absence of defensive armament rendered the aircraft very vulnerable to attack, and No. 600 Squadron's Blenheim Mk. Is were assigned as escort. The fact that the twin-engine fighter was itself at risk of lethal assault, given its mediocre performance as well as armament, was thankfully never tested even though the Luftwaffe was subsequently on theoretical hand as the Battle of France raged.

A Wellington based in the Suez Canal Zone that has been adapted to DWI operations is firmly dug into the sandy soil following a forced landing at El Ballah. It is serving with a GRU unit stationed at Ismailia. The distinctive nose and tail cones are clearly demonstrated, but the reason for the tethered camel's presence is unknown.

The expansion of the DWI fleet of aircraft beyond its then-current level seemed to have been sufficient to quell the risk of continued shipping losses, but it was the wholesale presence of Prof. Gauss's gear on Allied vessels that then led to the weapon's general suppression and the dispensing with the aerial countermeasure in UK waters. Attention was subsequently switched to the Mediterranean theater of operations. The mobile nature of the campaign, with ports such as Tobruk changing hands from Allied to Axis forces, clearly merited DWI operations on the occasions when the facilities were back in British hands. It was also ironic although inevitable that British mines were likely to be encountered, their delivery having naturally occurred during the Axis period of occupation! The DWI operations in this theater extended at least up to the enemy's expulsion from the North African landscape in May 1943. (A footnote to the creation of the engine/generator equipment indicates that what was titled DWI Mk. III was actually a cover for the later emergence of the Leigh Light.)

The dig-out has been satisfactorily completed and the bomber is photographed as it lifts off for the flight back to its airfield. Although the first four airframes were from Mk. 1A stock, a further eleven fitted with the Gypsy Six aero engines were adapted Mk. Is and designated DWI MK. II, as well as being fitted with the smaller 48-foot-diameter balsawood frame.

The Mk. 1C Wellington differed little if anything in outline compared to its Mk. 1A contemporary. One distinctive feature was the addition of the Lorenz blind-landing rod, which was positioned under the rear fuselage; the stub supports for this example on a No. 75 Squadron aircraft can just be discerned below the AA code letters. The variant would be a prominent element of the bombing offensive up to 1942.

Two Wellington variants from among the ultimately fourteen brought out would dominate the production scene, the first of which was the Mk. IC. The 2,685 airframes that were turned out would be largely split between Weybridge (1,052) and Chester (1,583), with the Blackpool plant contributing a figure of fifty. There was a subgroup of 138 airframes coming off the main plant's lines. These were converted to a torpedo-bomber function, with the specific release gear for the marine-launched missiles being installed; there was otherwise no external indication of the specialist machines' differentiation from the design's primary function as a bomber.

This number of Mk. ICs constituted marginally under 25 percent of the company's final output effort and was surpassed numerically only by the Mk. X (3,803). In addition, the Mark would be the last pure bomber variant to operate on the Pegasus, along with those airframes allocated to the GR Mk. VIII that would serve with Coastal Command. AUW would increase to 28,500 pounds, a factor that contrasted with a ceiling decrease of 3,600 feet and maximum speed by 10 mph compared to the Mk. I. Bombload capacity remained static at 4,500 pounds. The choice of the Pegasus XVIII radial engine, rated at 1,050 hp, proved to be a sound measure, but there was a potentially serious problem should power be reduced through the loss of one; what added to the problem was difficulty in feathering the DH propellers. The combined power loss and drag from the offending blades could easily lead to an inability to remain on a steady flight path.

The permanent deletion of the FN9 ventral turret occurred with the introduction of the Mk. IC on the production line; the absence of the several-hundred-pound turret weight added to the aircraft's overall speed and maneuverability. In addition, the switch to regular nocturnal operations basically rendered the defensive unit redundant, at least until the advent of the mid-1943 introduction of *Schräge*

Musik (slanting music) upward-angled cannon, with the tail gunners playing a key role in guarding the bomber from lethal attention.

Assault from a lateral angle was now responded to by the insertion of a Plexiglas panel just ahead of the wing trailing edge, which accommodated either a Vickers gas-operated (VGO) "K" machine gun with hundred-round ammunition pans or a Browning belt-fed equivalent. In practice, trials with the VGO led to the latter weapon being favored. Although welcome in further beefing up all-around cover, the degree of attack from this direction was seemingly not nearly as prevalent in the night skies over Europe compared to fore-and-aft passes.

A measure to improve the azimuth capability of the FN5 nose turret ironically brought with it a marginal increase in the bomber's instability. The area behind the turret was cut down and reshaped; this adjustment resulted in the turret protruding into the slipstream when fully traversed, an action that in turn created turbulence. This contrasted with the tight fit of the turret mounted on the Mk. IA, whose shape remained in line with the fuselage during the same maneuver. A ventral Lorenz receiving aerial was added, which comprised a horizontally aligned rod positioned marginally to the left of the fuselage centerline. The blind landing equipment linked to the aerial was largely but not comprehensively applied to the Mk. IC, while some Mk. IAs were retrospectively outfitted.

R1515 was one of a Mk. 1C production run of 550 turned out during 1940–41. The bomber, unlike most of her contemporaries, did not fly operationally. Instead, assignment to the Aircraft and Armaments Experimental Establishment (AAEE) was followed by duties with No. 104 OTU. Rebuilt as a B Mk. IV, it was involved in a takeoff crash in Northern Ireland during December 1943.

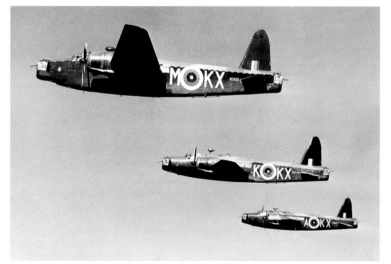

Airmen from another Nazi-occupied country, Czechoslovakia, are represented in this view of three Mk. 1Cs. No. 311 Squadron was formed in July 1940 and operated within Bomber Command until transfer to Coastal Command in April 1942. The Lorenz blind-flying rods are visible under KX: M and KX: K, but its absence on the far-side bomber indicates it is a Mk. 1A; however, its serial T2561 confirms it is actually a Mk. 1C.

The hydraulic system was redesigned, which entailed using VSG pumps and installing a 24-volt electrical system, from which a DR compass operated; the latter aid was a welcome if surprisingly late-day inclusion, given that its benefit both to the pilot and even more so to his navigator as a basic aid to tracking a safe and accurate flight path was of paramount importance.

Production commenced at Weybridge in the early spring of 1940, with one hundred R-prefixed-serial airframes turned out by June; a further three hundred T-prefixed batch covered the ensuing nine-month spell up to February. Chester was on stream during August with a large initial R-prefixed-serial batch of 550, whose construction spanned the ensuing nine months. Bomber Command's ranks were to be well stocked with the bomber. Unfortunately, at this stage of World War II the bombing offensive was advancing very fitfully and, in retrospect, doing so in a sadly inefficient manner vis-à-vis its goal of hammering the enemy's industrial and military potential into the ground.

The availability of onboard electronic equipment with which to track down even a target city or town, let alone deliver a bombload with any degree of accuracy, was steadily being developed as 1940 passed into 1941. However, this key limitation to striking effectively was further increased by the dispatch of bombers singly and in marginal numbers to any briefed target, which not only left the individual aircraft and crew wide open to specific interdiction by night fighters; the available bomb tonnage was unlikely to inflict any, let alone a serious, degree of punishment, and that was assuming it was accurately released.

The night-fighter threat was already gaining ground within the initial months of the offensive's inception. General Josef Kammhuber was creating aerial boxes backed by radar sites along the length of western Europe from Denmark to Belgium. Bf 110s and later Ju 88s would orbit an assigned "box" and be guided onto a bomber via a combination of two Würzburg sets, with one each tracking the night fighter and its prey. Once in range of its onboard radar set, the pilot would close in on and engage his target. Backing the burgeoning threat aloft were massive bands of searchlights and flak batteries, the latter also becoming increasingly radar directed.

The initial breakthrough in providing the crews with more-accurate navigation means was pioneered by the Mk. ICs of No. 115 Squadron during 1941. Three ground transmitters located at 100-mile intervals sent out a combined train of pulses in a set order. The navigator was equipped with a special radio receiver that enabled him to measure the time difference between receipt of the pulses. Reference of the differences to a special GEE map of Europe enabled him to determine his position, albeit with a precise accuracy gap of up to 6 miles. The maximum range of GEE was 400 miles,

A forward-directed view within what is stated to be a Mk. 1C provides an excellent view of the aircraft's geodetic framework. The circular flare chute is seen on the right opposite the Elsan chemical toilet. The Plexiglas bomb bay inspection panels are directly below, while the circular shape directly behind the bomb bay provides access for the function of the now-redundant ventral turret. The heavy pair of curved transverse frames to which the secondary wing spars are attached stand out as light shapes.

A trolley line of bombs is lined up alongside R1006, a Mk. 1C operating with No. 301 (Pomeranian) Squadron, a Polish unit. The bomber's operational career was very brief because it made a heavy belly landing at Swinderby upon return from what was its first sortie. Transfer to Nos. 21 and 18 OTUs followed before the aircraft caught fire at Bramcote in February 1942. The wavy camouflage separation line was applied on Bomber Command Wellingtons during this stage of World War II.

Several bomb-laden trolleys are displayed in front of a Mk. 1C whose bomb bay doors have been opened for the lethal load to be swallowed up. The barren winter scene with rows of leafless trees is typical of the conditions under which the ground crew will struggle to maintain their charges in perfect airworthy condition. The landing-light apertures are visible under the port wing.

The VR code letters just visible of this Mk. 1C confirm the bomber is serving with No. 419 (Moose) Squadron, a Royal Canadian Air Force (RCAF) unit. The mainly transatlantic personnel on hand would probably regard a British winter as mild in its effect compared to their experience back home. Absence of armament indicates the aircraft is not on immediate operational readiness.

Mk. 1C R1090's pilot has carried off a basically successful crash landing in respect of the overall airframe integrity; the sturdy nature of the geodetic structure should see the Wellington restored to airworthy condition. This specific "Wimpy" is recorded as serving with four OTUs between 1941 and its being "struck off charge" (SOC) in August 1944. An airbag to lift the bomber back onto its landing gear is seen outboard of the port engine.

A debriefing session at Feltwell during the initial operational period of 1940–41 is casual in layout compared to later in World War II. The airmen relaxing in chairs around a single table would be replaced by each crew undergoing interrogation at individual tables. This was necessary, given the huge increase in aircraft and crew establishment compared to the equivalent material and human resources seen here at this initial stage of the offensive.

The winter weather patterns are not letting up as a party of ground crew serving with No. 419 "Moose" Squadron and its Mk. 1Cs remove a tarpaulin from the wing, a measure intended to prevent ice accretion building up and robbing these vital surfaces of lift. The danger of slipping off what was a height of at least 10 feet and suffering injury or death was ever present in such climatic conditions.

Mk. 1C X9764, named "Rocky," has somewhat lived up to its name when its pilot carried off a risky albeit intact crash landing in a grove of young saplings. It was assigned in mid-1941 to No. 75 Squadron but later transferred to No. 304 (Silesian) Squadron, a Polish-staffed unit, with whom it was declared MIA on April 6 the following year.

Incendiary containers and 250-pound bombs are casually scattered under a Wellington. The outer bomb cells have two doors each, with the central cell being limited to one hinged on the port longitudinal beam. The navigation/identification light is mounted ahead of the crew entrance hatch, while the venturi for the blind-flying panel is fitted in line with the light and to the left of the hatch. The stick shapes protruding above the starboard door are winching rods to which crank handles will be attached when raising bombs into the aircraft.

A more comprehensive view of the damaged No. 149 Squadron Wellington demonstrates the structural integrity of Barnes-Wallis's geodetic framework. Note the twin navigation lights positioned on the rudder's upper rim. Also, note what looks like a hole, likely caused by a cannon shell that fortunately left Sgt. Billington physically intact from its explosive effect.

F/O Gregory (right) and Sgt. Billington, pilot and rear gunner of Mk. 1C OJ: A/X9746, examine the damage incurred during a raid on Duisburg on August 18, 1941. Cannon shells set the aircraft on fire around the tail area, and over the ensuing fifteen minutes, Billington, using his hands and even his parachute pack, fought and ultimately extinguished the blaze despite being drenched by hydraulic fluid released from the turret mechanism. Immediate DFC and DFM awards were granted to Gregory and Billington, respectively.

The final 1,000-bomber raid on Bremen (June 26, 1942) was expensive in losses, one of which was Mk. 1C Z1479/GR: A. The No. 301 (Polish) Squadron bomber lies on a sandbank near Dornumergrade, with two German servicemen straddling the cockpit. All the crew survived as POWs following flak strikes from the 8th Motorized Flak Division gun battery, the bomber being recorded as this unit's thirty-fourth kill (Abschüss).

Mk. IC R1333 was built at the Broughton Chester factory, one out of 550 produced between August 1940 and May 1941. It became a presentation aircraft whose cost was subscribed to by the management and staff. Unfortunately, its delivery to No. 99 Squadron in November culminated in a crash that saw it reduced to Category E or "written off." The wavy, midfuselage, camouflage separation line is unusual.

Mk. 1C R1697/NZ: C has returned from a raid with this large patch of canvas torn from its lower fin; the overall damage scale arising from the sortie must have been greater for the pilot—presumably the airman standing on the left of the picture—to bring off a crash landing. No. 304 (Polish) Squadron flew the Wellington within Bomber Command between November 1940 and May 1942, before being transferred to Coastal Command.

A tree-fringed dispersal at Mildenhall, current home for No. 149 Squadron, sees a Mk. 1C Wellington being wound up to full power by the airman in the cockpit. What appears to be directional signals by his companion's upraised arms is not a logical interpretation, since the bomber is firmly held in place by the wheel chocks.

The airfield facilities on Malta were rather primitive compared to their UK equivalents, there being marginal hangar space available. In addition, the proximity of the island to Sicily meant the defenders were under constant assault. In this picture a bomb bursting in the vicinity of a No. 104 Squadron Mk. 1C would see the airframe fortunate to escape serious damage. The general lack of protected dispersals added to the risk of damage or, worse still, destruction.

A senior NCO (*left*) is casting his eyes on the airmen working over a Mk. 1C serving with No. 214 Squadron at Stradishall. The scene appears more set up for publicity purposes than for the aircraft, since the average number assigned to each RAF bomber for maintenance work was half that seen in this photograph.

A sizable number of RAF bombers succeeded in making force landings on enemy territory. The action ensured the crew's survival but rendered the aircraft liable to examination by the Luftwaffe should its destruction not be carried out. A No. 99 Squadron Mk. 1C/T2501 has fallen into this unfortunate category as German personnel stand in the foreground. F/O Vivian and crew now became the latest involuntary "guests" of the Germans.

A pair of Mk. 1Cs are dispersed around the fringes of Mildenhall, both being No. 149 Squadron charges. The fin flash on the nearside bomber is almost invisible at the fin base compared to the rectangular pattern on the other aircraft; note the variation in fuselage roundel colors. The raising of the black undersides up the fuselage occurred during 1940–41. The towing vehicle is a Fordson design that was comprehensively used by the RAF during World War II.

and the closer the aircraft was to the signal sources, the greater the accuracy. The downside of its use was the Germans' ability to jam the signals with increasing effect the farther the aircraft flew away from the signal base; however, this negative countermeasure was delayed by several months through clever disinformation fed to the enemy even following evaluation of the equipment from an MIA bomber.

Supreme Award

During the July 7–8, 1941, attack on Münster, Mk. IC L7818 from No. 75 (RNZAF) Squadron was assailed from below by a Bf 110 during its homeward leg. Although the rear gunner on S/Ldr. Widdowson's crew sent the night fighter into a smoking dive, the cannon shell fusillade impacting at the juncture of the fuselage / starboard wing root set the bomber on fire within the inner wing section. The pilot, sensing the aircraft was fatally crippled, ordered a bailout but held back when second pilot Sgt. James Ward volunteered to extinguish the flames—by crawling out of the astrodome and onto the wing surface and blanking out the fire with the use of a canvas cover!

The seemingly suicidal attempt was nevertheless given the go-ahead, and the pilot throttled back to minimum safe speed to lessen the slipstream effect on Ward; even so, the icy blast would be difficult to withstand for more than a short period before numbing Ward's body, whereupon he would inevitably lose his hold and be swept away, and this was assuming he could even attain the aim of gaining access to the wing. Despite the daunting prospect of prompt failure, Ward, wearing his parachute and secured by a rope that his colleagues fed out behind him, managed to ease his way out via the astrodome and slither down the fuselage side and onto the wing. The fabric surfaces enabled him to do so by his kicking holes in the material, but even so it was a miracle that he had withstood the boreal gale's pressure effect.

Following several attempts to literally stuff the canvas bag in through the hole from where the flames, stoked from what was believed to be fuel from a split pipe, were emanating, his bid was successful, and the fire spluttered and finally cut out. Sure enough, his totally frozen condition was by now bearing down upon his bid to regain the bomber's interior, but his spirit of determination saw him succeed, and the pilot continued to maintain a course for what was a miraculous resurrection from an imminent fatal conclusion. The landing was made minus brake and flap operation, and the Wellington's fate was to be written off, such was the extent of the damage. Several weeks later, Ward attended Buckingham Palace to receive the Victoria Cross, the supreme military award

Christmas Day 1940 for the Czech crew operating on Mk. 1C L7788 saw them faced with one of their worst experiences after they force-landed on enemy soil, to endure over four years of captivity. The intact bomber has already had the fuselage roundel oversprayed with Luftwaffe insignia and will likely be flown to Rechlin or some other evaluation center.

being the sole example to be granted a Wellington crew member. Tragically, the twenty-two-year-old New Zealander's lease on life soon expired when, as the now first pilot on X3205, he was declared KIA over Hamburg the following September 16.

Mediterranean Operations

The Italian declaration of war in June 1940 caught the British ground forces and the RAF well off guard. In the case of the latter service, there were just a handful of squadrons operating on the Mk. I Blenheim, with restricted bombload capability. The Wellington provided a prompt form of reinforcement in what was the Mediterranean theater of operations (MTO), with the first unit, No. 70, at Kabrit in the Suez Canal zone converting onto the Mk. IC during September. Nos. 37 and 38 Squadron transited from the UK during November with their Mk. IAs, but these subsequently were displaced by the Mk. IC. The island of Malta was similarly, albeit temporarily, reinforced in striking capability by No. 148 Squadron, which then moved to Egypt the following March. Finally, No. 108 Squadron was re-formed in Egypt during the following August and took on the Wellington.

The availability of color film from British sources was limited compared to either the USAAF or Luftwaffe. This sharp shot of a No. 149 Squadron Mk. IC being manhandled by the ground crew is taken at the unit's main World War II location of Mildenhall, Suffolk. The dapple effect of the fabric shows up on the fuselage top surface, while the camouflage separation line drops down to run along the lower rim of the extended Plexiglas frame.

The truncated forward fuselage and wings on an anonymous Wellington are lying close to a coastal strip and under inspection by two Heer or Luftwaffe servicemen. The absence of the rear fuselage prevents specific squadron allocation being revealed, nor can the circumstances of the bomber's loss—either through being shot down or perhaps ditched—be confirmed. It is hoped that some or all on board survived their aircraft's demise.

The scrub-littered North African desert forms the barren background to a Mk. IC that has force-landed following being shot up by a Luftwaffe night fighter. The photo angle unfortunately does not reveal the extent of the serious damage inflicted, since this was centered on the invisible bomber's starboard side. F/O Goodman informed the author of this fact when loaning the photograph. Note how the turret and cockpit are shielded from the intense heat by canvas sheets.

The holes gouged out of the wing surface on L7818 are mute evidence of the almost suicidal bravery displayed by Sgt. James Ward, second pilot on the No. 75 (RNZAF) Squadron Mk. IC. Bearing a canvas cover, he managed to climb out via the astrodome, hold on to the framework, and stuff the material into the gap, thus smothering the flames emitted by a fuel pipe, before crawling back into the fuselage. The Victoria Cross was awarded for his action, but he was killed soon after when the Wellington he was now in charge of was MIA over Hamburg.

No. 214 Squadron was one of the immediate prewar squadrons converting onto the Mk. I Wellington that were subsequently displaced by the Mk. IC, as seen in a 1940 view of R3209/BU: H. The pristine condition of the bomber reveals the upward extension of the black on the fuselage to leave a thin strip of Dark Earth / Dark Green on the top. The aircraft survived operations until December 8, when it failed to return from a sortie to Düsseldorf in the Ruhr.

A nonpowered slave fuel bowser that is under tow by a camouflaged vehicle resembling an armored car is parked alongside a Mk. IC Wellington on the strategic island of Malta in the Mediterranean. Custom-built equipment such as these were ever at a premium on the beleaguered island, with any destroyed examples difficult to replace in the face of the enemy's ability to interdict British cargo vessels attempting to run the gauntlet of aircraft, E-boats, and U-boats.

No. 311 Squadron was the sole Czechoslovakian representative within Bomber Command, and these three Mk. ICs were operating out of East Wretham, Norfolk, between 1941 and transfer out to Coastal Command in April 1942. Aircraft "A" and "M" were MIA during mid-1942, and KX: K crashed during a landing on March 18, 1941. Blacking-over of the white roundel segments was done to reduce the markings being picked up by enemy searchlight beams.

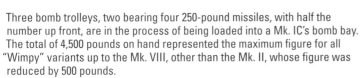

Three bomb trolleys, two bearing four 250-pound missiles, with half the number up front, are in the process of being loaded into a Mk. IC's bomb bay. The total of 4,500 pounds on hand represented the maximum figure for all "Wimpy" variants up to the Mk. VIII, other than the Mk. II, whose figure was reduced by 500 pounds.

The form of transport for this duo of RAF personnel is impractical, to say the least, but it provides a humorous aspect to the scene. The picture is believed taken at one of the staging points for aircraft being ferried from West Africa up to Egypt. The Wellington bears type C1 roundels, thus indicating a mid-1942 date onward.

A Vic of Mk. IC Wellingtons are holding a tight formation as they traverse a typically barren area somewhere on the North Africa landscape. The Vickers-Armstrong bomber was quickly on hand in this theater following Italy's June 1940 declaration of war and would prove an essential tool in carrying out raids against seaports, with Benghazi in Tripolitania (now Libya) a key target.

Any form of transport was welcome in wartime Britain, and the vehicle that is surrounded by a party of airmen believed assigned to No. 99 Squadron was more than welcome, even if its dimensions, given the number of potential passengers crowding around it, were minuscule to say the least.

An ominous sea change in Bomber Command's former inability to strike with high-capacity bombs was inaugurated over Emden on March 31–April 1, 1941. A No. 149 Squadron Mk. IC was one of two bombers modified to carry the 4,000-pound "Cookie" blast bomb. The aircraft's pilot was F/O J. H. Franks, who is the burly, mustachioed airman standing fifth from the right.

The mobile nature of the desert campaign's various battles, allied to the need to interdict the Axis convoy routes to North Africa, witnessed a partial or full deployment of the Wellingtons to Malta as well as Iraq, where a rebellion by the government supported by the Luftwaffe was quashed during mid-1941. The convoy strikes were backed up by sustained bombing attacks on the Axis seaports along the African coastline by the bombers stationed in Egypt. The ebb and flow of the ground campaigns gradually turned in the Allies' favor, with El Alamein's decisive success the catalyst for a steady but irresistible advance westward toward Tunisia, from where the Axis forces were cornered and forced to surrender in May 1943. The final victory was one in which the Wellington played a consistent role in hammering the enemy's land and seaborne facilities.

The creation of the Parachute Regiment in 1940 left the RAF with no custom-built designs in which to permit a swift delivery of the army personnel along with their support equipment, as later became the case with the arrival of the USAAF's C-46 and C-47. Instead, first the Armstrong-Whitworth Whitley and then the Mk. IC Wellington were marginally adapted to the role. In the case of the "Wimpy," the redundant ventral turret hatch was provided with a shallow metal rim protruding into the slipstream; the arrangement was meant to prevent the airflow from adversely affecting the soldier's emergence into midair. There was space for just a handful of the paratroopers, with a similar limitation on what could be carried in terms of support equipment.

The Mk. IC among aircraft that served in the Mediterranean theater of operations found itself serving in a secondary but important support role. In this instance the Wellington concerned is assigned to the Middle East Training School, based at El Kabrit in the Suez Canal Zone. All armament has been detached from the turrets.

MK. IC WELLINGTON SPECIFICATIONS

Wingspan	86 ft., 2 in.
Length	64 ft., 7 In.
Height	17 ft., 5 in
All-up weight	28,500 lbs.
Power plant	Pegasus VXII, 1.150 hp radial engine

Armament

FN5 nose turret with two. 303 machine guns
FN10 rear turret with two. 303 machine guns
Two fuselage beam-mounted. 303 machine guns

Performance

Max speed	235 mph
Service ceiling	18,000 ft.
Range	2,550 miles
Bombload	4,500 lbs.
Crew	6 (later reduced to 5)

The training of volunteers for Britain's Parachute Regiment was initially conducted via the Whitley and Wellington. In this picture, several men equipped with the original "pillbox" helmets are embarking into a Mk. IC. They will jump through the original ventral turret aperture seen in the background, thanks to the raised circular frame placed around the perimeter, which ensures the men will make a clean exit.

The latest Wellington variant to take to the skies was the sole example to make a comprehensive switch from a radial to an in-line engine; in this case the choice fell upon the Rolls-Royce Merlin X, with a power output of 1,145 hp. The reason for the change was reportedly due to the possibility of a shortfall in Pegasus engines; this rationale is open to challenge, especially in light of the subsequent availability of the Bristol Hercules. As matters stood, the Merlin was to prove a sound and arguably superior choice compared to its Bristol contemporary. The one weakness with in-line designs compared to radials was an inability to continue operating should the glycol tank be punctured.

The prototype was the thirty-eighth production Mk. I, L4250, an airframe that would later be utilized for testing the dorsal-mounted Vickers 40 mm cannon. First flown in March 1939, the production lines at Weybridge provided the sole source for the 410 airframes involved. A structural alteration involved the tailplane, which was expanded to provide an improvement in stability. Internal alterations concerned cabin heating, although the relatively uncompartmented fuselage interior would have proved a severe challenge to crew comfort in this respect; another addition involved 300 pounds of turret hydraulic gear. The engines now featured Rotol propellers with wooden Jablo blades. Defensive armament remained at the same level, with FN5 nose and FN10 rear turrets as well as single-beam guns in triangular-shaped Plexiglas panels. The absence of ventral cover was to evolve as a constant problem for the Wellington, and indeed for its twin- and four-engine contemporaries, right throughout World War II.

The bomb calibers within Bomber Command were beginning to assume expanded size and explosive effect as early as 1940–41, when the Mk. II entered service. The 4,000-pound "Cookie" blast bomb first became available in the new year, and it fell to several examples of the Vickers variant to have their bomb bays modified in order to carry the massive cylinder; the first recorded operational use involved Nos. 9 and 149 Squadron on March 31–April 1 over Emden.

The need to build up a bomber force with which to challenge the operations of the Axis powers in North Africa had witnessed the dispatch of Mk. IA– and Mk. IC–equipped squadrons to that theater during the early stage of the campaign, and their numbers were now added to by the Mk. II. The range capability of the "Wimpy" ensured that the major enemy seaports along the Mediterranean coastline were kept under steady assault. As operational events transpired, the Wellington was to constitute the main heavy-bomber presence for the RAF until the arrival of the USAAF B-24 Liberator during 1942, a design that was also destined to be operated by several RAF squadrons within the theater up to VE-day.

The future displacement of propeller- by jet-turbine-powered aircraft was already established in Germany two years prior to the British following suit. Air Commodore Frank Whittle's long fight to convince the Air Ministry that the propulsion source was an absolute necessity if the RAF were to advance in terms of enhanced-quality aircraft designs was finally accepted. At least three Mk. II Wellingtons played a part in the overall development plans. Their rear turrets were detached, and a streamlined "cone" covered the W2B/23 fitted to Z8570/G; Z5389/G bore a BTH W2B, and W5518/G a W2/700. The latter duo also featured extra wing panels that extended these to 60 feet, while power was provided by the Merlin 62, with an added output of 155 hp over the Merlin X.

A switchover from radial to in-line engine power was made on the Wellington Mk. II; this took the form of the Merlin X, rated at 1,145 hp. The airframe chosen for the installation was L4251, but tests proved unsatisfactory regarding C of G stability. This key problem affecting flight characteristics was cured by the increase in tailplane span and elevator mass balance.

A rearward-angled view of the Mk. II test airframe reveals the original Mk. I status of L4251 thanks to the twin radio masts and unfaired D/F loop. A second indication of its vintage is the retention of the prewar roundel pattern, which was superseded by type A1 and B alternatives by 1940. The bomber never flew on operations since it was assigned in turn to the Royal Aircraft Establishment (RAE), followed by the Aircraft and Armament Experimental Establishment (AAEE).

The displacement of the radial Pegasus engine by the bulkier Rolls-Royce Merlin presents the "Wimpy" with a more pugnacious albeit less streamlined appearance. The port motor on a Mk. II assigned to No. 405 (Vancouver) Squadron, the first within a large group of RCAF units serving in Bomber Command, is wound up at full bore. Camouflage pattern on the upper fuselage is restricted to a relatively narrow strip.

Z8345, a Mk. II operating with No. 104 Squadron, is seen overflying the British countryside sometime during the latter half of 1941. The bomber displays the triangular window structure, which permitted the mounting of a machine gun. Note how the aircraft letter intersects the serial. EP: R was written off in a crash at LG 121 on June 4, 1942, following the squadron's transfer to North Africa.

The four 250-pound bombs being guided toward the gaping bomb bay on a No. 405 Squadron Mk. II constitute one-quarter of the bomber's maximum carrying capacity of 4,000 pounds. The narrow confines of the bay prevented the carriage of individual weapons above the 2,000-pound slim-shaped, armor-piercing bomb, but modifications to some airframes enabled the 4,000-pound "Cookie" to be carried.

No. 12 Squadron's involvement with the Wellington was concentrated wholly on the Mk. II between November 1940 and November 1942, after which it switched to the Lancaster. The snow-strewn and bleak airfield on which the unit is seen here is either Binbrook or the subsequent and final World War II Lincolnshire location of Wickenby.

No. 214 Squadron, based at Stradishall within No. 3 Group, took on the Mk. II, albeit in relatively few numbers, during 1941. The need to modify the Wellington's bomb bay with its trio of narrow longitudinal cells, in order to carry the "Cookie," was carried out on some Mk. ICs along with five Mk. IIs, the latter currently assigned to No. 214 Squadron. W5442 was the second within the quintet to be so modified. The tiger's-head artwork and "SRI GUROH" title refer to the unit's adoption by the Federated Malay States.

No. 405 (RCAF) Squadron was one of that nation's squadrons to convert onto the Mk. II. The forward element of the fuselage's Plexiglas frame has been blacked out around the edges, while the rectangular window behind the FN5 turret is totally covered up. The "horse and plough" duo provide a rather peaceful contrast with the aerial instrument of war. Many airfields were located on former farmland, and the areas between the runways and perimeter tracks were often cultivated to provide vital food supplies for the population.

During April 1941, No. 104 Squadron was re-formed at Driffield, Yorkshire, where the crews were introduced to the Wellington. Mk. II EP: R/W5461 is caught on camera overflying a rather flat landscape, typical of England's eastern regions. The bomber displays evidence of operational tiredness as cast up by the worn wing leading edges, and the national markings are dulled down. Bomber was MIA over Berlin the following August 12–13.

The presence of two Mk. II Wellingtons, one on final landing approach and the other taxiing round the perimeter track, still does not diminish the pastoral nature of the backdrop to these modern instruments of warfare. The unit is the RCAF's No. 405 Squadron, which operated out of Topcliffe in North Yorkshire. Note the shallow curving camouflage separation line on the ground-bound bomber.

A trio of No. 405 Squadron Mk. II Wellingtons squat on their dispersals; they are probably loaded up and ready for their latest foray into the ever-deadly nocturnal skies over Europe that are their natural environment.

Z5897 is taxiing out from its dispersal at Kabrit in the Suez Canal Zone on December 3, 1942. The absence of No. 104 Squadron's normal EP code letters was a regular feature on bombers in the North Africa operational theater. This Mk. II was MIA over the island of Pantellaria the following June 11. Note the B-24D in the left background.

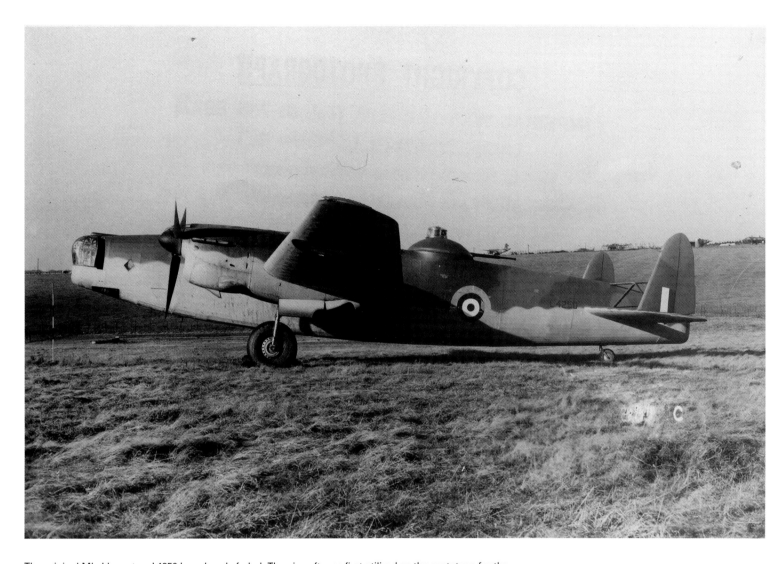

The original Mk. I layout on L4250 has sharply faded. The aircraft was first utilized as the prototype for the Merlin-powered Mk. II. A further structural disfigurement has occurred here, with the dorsal fin being replaced by twin units applied out on the stabilizers. The change was caused by air-flow disturbance from the turret adversely affecting directional stability.

A rear-angle view of the much-modified L4250 seen in the previous photo reveals a much more standard layout apart from the rear turret, which has been faired over. The 40 mm armed turret structure with its single weapon and offset cupola presents an unaerodynamic image, and the experiment did not advance beyond this stage of evaluation.

A final view of the modification to L4250 confirms the offset nature of the turret gunner's viewing cupola, the airflow therefrom disturbing the pilot's lateral control of the bomber, and the attendant need for the revised twin-fin structure. Picture angle also reveals the horizontal bracing rods between the fins.

In April 1941, No. 104 Squadron converted from Ansons to the Mk. II Wellington at Driffield, where it remained until February 1942, when it transferred to North Africa. A train of 250-pound bomb-laden trolleys are destined for EP: K, squatting in the background.

The Mk. II Wellington played a regular part in the conduct of the North African campaign and inevitably bore its share of overall RAF losses. In this instance, an anonymous bomber has suffered a fractured central fuselage following what was probably a heavy crash landing that has also dislodged the starboard Merlin.

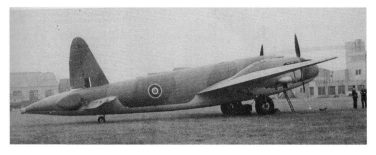

Three Mk. II Wellingtons were used to test the first British jet engines based on Sir Frank Whittle's design. This is W5389/G (the letter denoting an experimental function), which bore a W2B engine positioned in the extended tail cone. The bulged teardrop shape below the fin and rudder has an inlet at the front through which air is drawn. The aircraft bore extended wings and Merlin 60 engines.

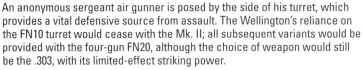

An anonymous sergeant air gunner is posed by the side of his turret, which provides a vital defensive source from assault. The Wellington's reliance on the FN10 turret would cease with the Mk. II; all subsequent variants would be provided with the four-gun FN20, although the choice of weapon would still be the .303, with its limited-effect striking power.

A W2/700 jet is mounted in the tail of another of the test vehicle Mk. IIs, in this case W5518/G. In contrast to its companion test beds, whose air intakes were at the front of the pod, this aircraft's orifices were flush-mounted. The rectangular panels form the securing base for the tail cone.

CHAPTER 6
Mk. III

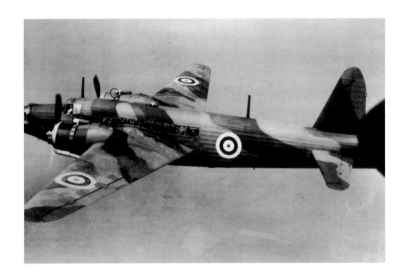

The original Mk. I outline of L4251 has undergone little external change, with the retention of twin radio masts and unfaired D/F loop, although FN power turrets have replaced the inefficient Vickers units. The major change is the installation of the Hercules power source in place of the Pegasus; the aircraft is acting as a test vehicle for the Bristol design that will power the Wellington Mk. III.

To date, the Wellington had been powered either by the Bristol Pegasus or the Rolls-Royce Merlin. The company's link to radial design would now be resurrected in terms of the former-named concern, with the Hercules the choice. Once again, a Mk. I airframe (L4251) was selected for engine tests, with the Hercules HEISM fitted with two-stage superchargers along with DH "Bracket"-type propellers the choice. Unsatisfactory results accruing from flight testing brought a second aircraft into the experimental arena, Mk. IC R9238; this time a pair of Hercules III motors with Rotol electric propellers were fitted, with positive overall performance results. Also applied in place of the FN10 tail turret was the four-gun FN20A, the result being a doubling of firepower, although with the .303 weapon still in place. The FN21A ventral turret, which had first been mooted for the Mk. III, was accordingly not taken up. Deicing equipment, barrage balloon cutters, and windscreen wipers were also added.

Both power plants were rated at 1,425 hp, but the Hercules III would be supplanted by the XI as production advanced at Chester and Blackpool to an overall figure of 1,519. One external difference with the Pegasus was the presence of a short-length carburetor air filter above the cowling/nacelle joint. Although overall performance in maximum speed and range was inferior to the Mk. II, for example, the variant would serve as the main prosecutor of the bombing offensive in the twin-engine category following entry into service with No. 9 Squadron in June 1941. Within the next fifteen months, both the Hampden and Whitley would cease bomber operations and be transferred out to other commands; the Wellington, by contrast, would soldier on for just over one more year before its withdrawal occurred.

The original design for training paratroop forces was the Whitley, and this policy was extended further to the Wellington

A second Wellington, in this case Mk. IA P9238, was used to test the Hercules III with an electric Rotol propeller, a combination displacing the original Hercules HEISM with two-stage superchargers and DH propeller, which proved unsatisfactory in performance. As with L4251, so this aircraft was retained for work with the AAEE, followed by transfer to the RAE. The low camouflage separation line is typical of the overall spray pattern on early Mk. IAs.

A second major change in power for the Wellington arrived with the Mk. III, the power being switched back to a radial-designed source, with the Bristol Co.'s Hercules in place of the Pegasus. Wellington Z1572 is seen assigned to No. 419 (Moose) Squadron but is recorded as having had prior service with Nos. 115 and 75 (RNZAF) Squadrons. The RCAF unit flew the variant during most of 1942 before transferring onto the Halifax.

in the shape of the Mk. III, beginning with X3268. A large yoke bracket was applied to the ventral fuselage behind the bomb bay to enable a glider to be towed; the stress factor of the attachment was established at a maximum of just under 16,000 pounds, a level that allowed the towing of the RAF's standard glider, the Airspeed Horsa. Ten soldiers were carried along with containers holding up to 350 pounds of weight in all.

One Mk. III, BJ895, had its bomb bay interior altered to accommodate two golf-ball-shaped missiles that earned the nickname thanks to retaining the mass of shallow dimples applied to the real sporting sphere. These were used to test the efficacy of successfully destroying solid structures such as the several major dams that No. 617 Squadron would assault. Although the explosively inert missiles did function properly, their round outline was later replaced by the cylindrical pattern of the Upkeep weapons used during the May 1943 assault.

A Wellington serving within the SEAC theater of operations is fully loaded up with a combination of bombs and incendiaries canisters, the latter mounted in the starboard bay. The two longitudinal beams cutting the overall bay into three subsections had the effect of limiting the maximum individual bomb size that could be accommodated therein to a 250-pound level.

A large group of what is almost wholly composed of aircrew members, two of whom (*front row*) are fully kitted up for flying, are posed in front of one of the equally anonymous squadron's Mk. III Wellingtons. The officer standing second from left wears an Army-pattern peaked hat and jacket distinctly different from his colleagues' outfits, which seems to match the examples worn by members of the South African Air Force (SAAF).

KO: P/ X3662 was one of 450 Mk. III airframes produced and delivered between May 1941 and July 1942. The bomber bears an impressive number of ops markings, totaling thirty-six, and indeed did survive operations before transferring to No. 20 OTU. It was fated to be ditched off the Isle of Skye on October 8, 1943.

The huge hole gouged out of a Wellington Mk. III's rear fuselage would almost certainly have proved fatal to the aircraft's survival had it involved a standard airframe borne by most RAF bombers. Instead, the crisscross geodetic pattern has enabled the pilot to maintain control and land the aircraft at East Wretham, Norfolk. The squadron identity is unknown, as is the date of the incident.

No. 425 (Alouette) Squadron's KW: E/X3763 demonstrates how the RDM2 matte black paint tended to peel off under the slipstream effect, as seen on the vertical fin; the shade was replaced by a glossier version with superior adhesive qualities. The No. 6 (Canadian) Group bomber was lost over Stuttgart on April 14–15, 1943, by which time the individual letter had changed to "L."

Wellingtons were the mainstay of a sizable number of nonoperational training units. In this case a line of Mk. IIIs are arrayed around the perimeter track at Hixon in central England. An AEC fuel bowser is in the process of filling up the tanks on BK347.

The original adaptation of the Wellington's bomb bay for the bomber to carry the "Cookie" was applied to the Mk. IC. In this case the three airmen pushing the laden trolley toward a "Wimpy" reveals the aircraft as being a Mk. III. This is confirmed by the supercharger air cooler on the cowling of what is a Hercules engine; the Mk. III was the first variant to transfer from the Pegasus to this radial successor also produced by the Bristol Co.

Mk. III BJ895's forward bomb bay contains two spheroid shapes whose exterior resembles the pitted surface of a golf ball. The missiles were used to test the use of similar-shaped weapons, with a view to destroying solid structures such as barrage dams and with the major examples in western Germany the goal. Tests were conducted off Chesil Beach in southeastern England, which culminated with successful penetration of the Möhne and Eder Talsperre (Dams), albeit not with these weapons.

As the war progressed, the bulk of Wellington final production from the Mk. III onward took place away from the parent location at Weybridge. The fuselage, with almost all the fabric in place, is seen at Hawarden near Chester and shows the triangular Plexiglas frame for the beam guns, a feature first standardized on the Mk. III. The converse reduction in production at Weybridge granted more emphasis on research and development by the staff.

CHAPTER 7

Mk. IV

To date, all production variants of the Wellington had operated under British power sources in the form of the Bristol Pegasus, Bristol Hercules, or Rolls-Royce Merlin. The Mk. IV, by contrast, would be powered by a non-British equivalent. The original decision to solicit support from the American government for the manufacture of the Pratt & Whitney Double Wasp radial had been made as early as 1939. Negotiations proved somewhat protracted, because it was several months before the US authorities finally agreed to the dispatch of two engines—an act that could have been redundant in the face of the Air Ministry's imminent plan to abandon the project. What likely tipped the scales in favor of continuing with the scheme was the danger of British manufacturing facilities being overwhelmed as the conflict expanded, and rendering production incapable of matching up to operational demands.

Chester-built R1220 was chosen as the model test aircraft for what was the R-1830-S3C4-C engine, rated at 1,050 hp, and test flights commenced, albeit not until the following December. Hamilton Standard propellers were applied, but the excessive noise level they broadcast witnessed their replacement by the quieter-functioning Curtiss electric equivalent. Carburetor failure that induced R1220 to suffer a heavy crash landing during its approach to Weybridge's runway did not delay the arrival of several Mk. IVs to Boscombe Down, where an overall evaluation found the aircraft passing the operational test; in addition, flight testing if not also release testing of the Lindholme lifeboat was indulged in by one among this group. The factory at Chester commenced production of what constituted a 185-strong Z-prefix serial batch in June 1941, the run being completed the following March.

Despite entering service after the Mk. III, the new Mark's structure was essentially akin to the Mk. IC, down to the retention

R1220 was produced as a Mk. 1C at the company's Chester factory but never saw active operations, being assigned to the AAEE. The aircraft became the prototype for the Mk. IV, the sole external difference being the Pratt & Whitney Twin Wasp engines, which displaced the Bristol Pegasus.

A second, more lateral view of R1220 picks out the small air intake atop the cowling, which contrasts with the Pegasus's lack of a similar facility; this was the single obvious external difference compared to a standard Mk. IC airframe.

of the FN5 and FN10 two-gun turrets. However, some airframes were adapted to bear the four-gun FN20A in the rear location. There were reports that some airframes dispensed with the fuselage window length but still retained the necessary location for the beam-mounted guns' Plexiglas diamond or the subsequent triangular equivalent on the Mk. III onward, which provided the necessary visual requirement for the gunners. Although overall flight performance matched that of the Mk. III, there was one notable improvement: this was due to the Mk. IV Double Wasp engines, which provided a maximum speed of 299 mph, an increase of 44 mph over the previous variant.

The August 1941 delivery of the first aircraft was to Nos. 300 and 301 (Polish) Squadrons, followed by No. 458 (RAAF) Squadron; by November, two more units, Nos. 142 and 460 (RAAF) Squadrons, were similarly equipped, and the last to convert was No. 305 (Polish) Squadron, although this was not until the following August. A seventh nonbomber squadron introduced to the Mk. IV was No. 544 (PR), whose crews indulged in experimental nocturnal sorties over Britain up to early 1943, when the more suitable Mosquito took over the duty.

The Mk. IV was introduced to operations during what was the 1941–42 period, when Bomber Command experienced a hiatus from being a clearly failing entity to one that could advance the purpose of the offensive in a positive and ultimately irresistible manner. By the time the final sorties were being flown by the three Polish squadrons during the first half of 1943—the other squadrons having already done so—the Battle of the Ruhr was in full swing, and the Wellington was playing a full part in that key campaign to punish the manifold factory complexes within that massive geographic zone.

R1515 was another of a handful of Mk. ICs from a 550-airframe batch built by Vickers' Chester factory that were converted to a B Mk. IV standard. As with R1220, this Wellington was also retained by the AAEE before transfer to No. 104 OTU; the bomber crashed during takeoff at Mullaghmore on December 20, 1943. The aircraft has still to be converted to the Pratt & Whitney engines.

CHAPTER 8
Mk. V/VI

A basic operational question exercising the minds of the Bomber Command hierarchy and, by extension, that of bomber design staff was how to circumvent the German fighter and flak defensive network without suffering prohibitive losses. As the bombing offensive developed, so the situation grew steadily worse as 1941 progressed. By then, the crews had no option but to fly a direct course to their targets in western Europe; the ability to fly divergent courses, particularly in a southern arc, placed too much pressure on fuel reserves. The alternative measure would be to literally fly out of reach of the opposition, but the RAF bombers on hand possessed no ability to do so and indeed would in practice never achieve this goal throughout the course of World War II.

However, during the late prewar period, the possibility of achieving this goal had been met by Vickers, which carried out work that culminated in the appearance during 1940 of two Wellington prototypes, powered by the Bristol Hercules. Granted a Mk. V status, IC R3298 mounted the Hercules III with a 1,425 hp rating, while Mk IC / Mk. VI R3299 was fitted with the uprated 1,600 hp Hercules VIII (a third power source under consideration was the Hercules XI, which utilized GEC exhaust-driven turbo blowers, and this was subsequently tested on R3298). One more variant involved W5796, which would feature the Hercules VIII as its power source and would be regarded as the Mk. V production aircraft. However, the trio would represent the total out of twelve intended Mk. V airframes; W5795 was the first to be fitted with the Merlin 60 and acted as the first production Mk. V1, only to suffer a crash.

The prototype R3298 first took to the air as the Battle of Britain was reaching its climax in September, with an overall outline that was not totally at variance with the "Wimpy's" normal outline other than in the drastically amended forward fuselage. The stepped-down area between the cockpit and nose turret was totally erased. In its place was a continuation of the top fuselage line, which possessed a bubble Plexiglas frame for the pilot. The underside from the bomb bay sloped upward in a curve to about midfuselage height. There it matched with the lower edge of a cone-pattern nose panel similar to that of a clown's nose; an ovoid Plexiglas panel for the bomb aimer was inserted in the cone's lower curve.

The major internal alteration to the forward fuselage witnessed a deletion of several feet normally accommodating the bomb aimer's position, the front of which was closed off with a transverse and curved top geodetic panel; the fuselage side panels were also reduced in height back to the wing leading edges. Into this "cradle" was positioned the spheroid capsule, which was entered from the rear by the reduced complement of pilot, navigator / bomb aimer, and wireless operator and was pressurized to accommodate the anticipated substratospheric altitudes up to 36,000 feet that the bomber would theoretically attain. The ground pressure level of 10,000 feet equated to an internal 7 lbs. / in.^{2} maximum. Pilot visibility from the bubble, which was offset to port, was notably restricted, making for a tricky landing approach, but less so on takeoff; airframes beyond the seven original Mk. V and VI airframes were refitted with extended spherical Plexiglas equivalents.

High-altitude test flights revealed several basic problems arising from the extreme subzero temperatures. The pilot's canopy suffered from icing up, which was suspected as being due to cabin humidity. Grease solidified in the control hinge bearings, with the added-on effect of seized-up flight controls and trimmer circuits; also affected were the bomb bay doors and rear turret. Oil content was also affected; during one flight, frozen lumps of oil were cast out due to a suspected leak, the result being damage to the fuselage structure that these impacted. One critical failure involving crew security arose from ice accumulation on the fuselage, which hindered the opening of the door in the case of an emergency evacuation; the alternative was depressurizing the cabin—which took a full ten minutes to achieve! Air-conditioning and heating within the capsule were equally prone to failure, but in time these manifold limitations were at least partially but never completely resolved. The work on the pressurized Wellingtons also formed the basis for the equivalent facilities to be subsequently applied to PR Spitfires as well as to the Westland twin-engine Welkin, although this specific project never advanced beyond the prototype stage. The intention to manufacture a further nine pure Mk. Vs never materialized, however. A major restriction in the original Mk. VI production batch order resulted in only sixty-four out of the 120 aircraft being produced. There were two notable

The central core for the Mk. V/VI concept of ultrahigh-altitude flight involved the crew capsule. The gutting-out of the cockpit section was necessary for the forward fuselage structure to enclose the capsule, as seen in this view.

The skeletal fuselage frame in the preceding picture is now part of the almost fully assembled prototype Mk. V R3298 but still lacks its Hercules III engines. The gap between the curved front of the lower fuselage and base of the capsule is now enclosed as part of the overall fairing surrounding the capsule. The oval panel in the upper nose would be the sighting point for the bomb aimer.

changes from the Mk. V, the first change affecting the initial batch of airframes that switched to the Merlin 60 or 62; the 1,600 hp power plant proved to be a key factor in raising maximum speed to 300 mph, which was the peak of the Wellington's performance envelope in this category. Second, four broad-blade propellers replaced the three-blade units applied to the Mk. V. The wings were extended by 12 feet on W5800 and W5795, the extra lift boosting the aircraft's ability to sustain 40,000 feet in maximum altitude during high-altitude tests, but this was subsequently removed. It is unlikely that any other of the twenty-seven first Mk. VI airframes within the W5798-5818 and DR471-479 batch were similarly adapted. Crew complement rose to four; this was due to an official change to the original observer crew status, which covered bomb aiming and navigation; there now existed a separation of the twin duties formerly allotted to the aircrew involved, with volunteers now assuming either a bomb aimer or navigation role as their permanent solo function.

Tests at the RAE and Boscombe Down involved anticipated operations with the Sperry bombsight. In addition, thirty-two further Mk. VI airframes (DR481-483/G, 485-504/G, and 519-527/G) were assigned to an intended "Oboe" operational function. This duty was destined to remain moribund, however, due to the adaptation of the immeasurably superior-performing Mk. IV Mosquito. The latter's greater speed and particularly maneuverability granted it a far better chance of survival should it be intercepted, while the crew had no need to depend on a pressurized cockpit even while operating at altitudes not too far short of that enjoyed by the Mk. VI.

W5801 and W5802, from the original Mk. VI batch of twenty-seven, were reportedly allocated to No. 109 Squadron at Stradishall in March 1942, where they conducted special radio experiments; the latter aircraft later transferred to the RAE at Farnborough. Finally, DR480 and 484 had their bomb bays altered to accommodate the 4,000-pound "Cookie." However, as 1943 commenced, the operational need for the variants had disappeared, and the bulk of their number, having been assigned to maintenance units, now suffered the fate of being scrapped.

R3298 was the first of a planned twelve production Mk. V airframes, a figure later reduced to three. Power on this airframe was supplied by the Hercules III, but the other pair operated on either the Hercules XI or VIII. The offset, elliptical bubble canopy was replaced by a circular equivalent on Mk. V R3299 and all subsequent airframes up to Mk. VIA DR479, after which it was reintroduced on the remaining thirty-five airframes.

The second Mk. V prototype, Type 421/R3299, is revealed in the basic reconfiguration from its original Mk. 1C layout. The extended nose area, with a continuous upper fuselage line broken only by the pilot's elliptical canopy, is the major difference in the conversion project. This example switched from the first prototype R3298's use of the Hercules III and Hercules XI to the Hercules VIII. The yellow "P" denotes the aircraft's prototype status, as do the yellow undersides.

Only three Hercules-powered Mk. Vs were built prior to a switch to the Merlin on the remaining sixty-four airframes built out of the original order for 132. This is W5798, which was intended to be the first of twenty-seven Mk. V airframes converted to Mk. VIA status. Note the four-blade propellers applied to the series 60 engines. This airframe was one of two used in Sperry bombsight tests at RAE and Boscombe Down.

Only three Hercules-powered Mk. Vs were built prior to a switch to the Merlin on the remaining sixty-four airframes built out of the original order for 132. This is W5798, which was intended to be the first of twenty-seven Mk. V airframes converted to Mk. VIA status. Note the four-blade propellers applied to the series 60 engines. This airframe was one of two used in Sperry bombsight tests at RAE and Boscombe Down.

The overall outline of the high-altitude Wellington variant displays a porcine style compared to the standard airframe. The displacement of the radial Hercules by the series 60 Merlin identifies what is an anonymous example of a Mk. VI. Note how the Lorenz beam aerial had been moved farther back and to the starboard side of the aircraft's centerline.

DR494 was one of a further thirty-one airframes built as Mk. VIGs within a total of thirty-two turned out between May 1942 and January 1943. The original intention to apply armament had been dispensed with, and the rear turret displaced by a conical fairing. The function of these aircraft in an "Oboe" role was abandoned in favor of the Mosquito, and DR494 was one of all but eight destined to be "struck off charge" (SOC).

CHAPTER 9
Mk. X

The prototype Wellington X3595 shows off the more refined outline of the Bristol Hercules VI engines applied to the Mk. X. The aperture in the triangular fuselage window, which was utilized for a defensive armament supplement to the nose and tail FN turrets, is evident, although attack from this lateral angle was basically absent during nocturnal operations over the Third Reich at this stage of World War II. The bomber survived service with No. 75 Squadron as well as several second-echelon units and was SOC in 1945.

What was to be the final Wellington bomber variant to serve during the bombing offensive would be the sole one to extend its service into the 1950s. The Mk. X bore little external difference to the Mk. III, but the Hercules VI or XVI provided one clue. In place of the short-length carburetor air intake possessed by the Mk. III's Hercules III or XI engines, there appeared an extended version. The engines were fitted with an auto-operating system for the carburetors as well as a single lever control. The added weight of the airframe, whose AUW figure of 36,000 pounds was 1,500 pounds above its nearest contemporary, the Mk. III, was countered by the introduction of recently developed light alloy material that also equaled the durability of mild steel.

Not only was the performance of the Mk. X superior in relation to all its Wellington bomber contemporaries, it was also constructed in far-greater numbers, a total of 3,803 being turned out by the twin Vickers subfactories in Lancashire and Cheshire. A further tribute to its qualities was the fact that even when withdrawn from Bomber Command ranks in late 1943, its continued presence in the Italian and Far East (Burma) campaigns, where the variant carried out strategic operations alongside the Consolidated B-24 Liberator, was maintained right up until the end of hostilities in either theater.

A testament to the structural integrity of the geodetic layout arose from the incident involving Mk. X HE239 / NA: Y of No. 428 (Ghost) Squadron on March 3–4, 1943. The target at Duisburg was being overflown when a flak strike excised the FN20 rear turret and its hapless occupant, along with the lower surface of the rudder, as well as stripping a swathe of fabric from the fuselage. The elevators and the rudder thankfully remained intact; even so, what could have been a death blow turned into an ultimately successful bid by Sgt. L. F. Williamson not only to remain aloft but also to regain friendly soil and land the Wellington on the runway. The Distinguished Conduct Medal he was subsequently awarded was thoroughly earned.

A Wellington's latest and clearly final landing or takeoff maneuver has ended in total failure. The airframe has basically held together, although badly fractured behind the wings, so there is a good chance the crew survived the incident. The detached carburetor air-intake and oil-cooler sections in the foreground, in line with the two airmen as well as the "Bell" pattern propeller covers, indicate the variant is a Mk. X, while the visible code letters suggest a nonoperational unit such as an OTU.

A Mk. X gracefully surmounts the almost solid cloud formation as it trails the photographer's aerial platform. Points of note are the slim-line air intakes on the Hercules VI motors, the bell pattern spinner covers for the propellers, and the engine exhausts transferred to the inner cowling surfaces. The pitot mast protrudes below the starboard outer wing.

Minelaying was a key secondary element in Bomber Command operations, but the low-level nature of such operations was equally fraught with risk. Mk. X HE196, from No. 196 Squadron, has bellied in following a "Gardening" sortie to the Frisian Islands on March 14–15, 1943, the impact shattering the wooden Jablo propeller blades. The airbags are being inflated to bring the bomber up to landing-gear height, but the presence of a main wheel in the foreground, if coming from this aircraft, would appear to nullify any immediate attempt at movement.

A Mk. X that has probably been transferred to training duties, judging by the absence of unit code letters, has swerved off or overshot the runway; the resultant impact with the undulating terrain has fractured the fuselage, as seen in the first view. The second picture, taken from the front, shows how the nose turret, particularly the cockpit area, is twisted out of shape, leaving the pilot fortunate to escape injury or worse in the latter case.

A Mk. X that has probably been transferred to training duties, judging by the absence of unit code letters, has swerved off or overshot the runway; the resultant impact with the undulating terrain has fractured the fuselage, as seen in the first view. The second picture, taken from the front, shows how the nose turret, particularly the cockpit area, is twisted out of shape, leaving the pilot fortunate to escape injury or worse in the latter case.

The narrow bomb bay cells on the Wellington were custom-built for the carriage of sea mines, among other similar-shaped missiles. Two of these antishipping weapons are about to be loaded into BH: E/ HF598, a Mk. X assigned to No. 300 (Masovian) Squadron, a Polish air force unit. The parachute-assisted mines will be dropped off the European coast; the code name for this type of operation was "Gardening."

The process of refueling the starboard wing tanks on what is a Mk. X Wellington is being made via a slave fuel bowser, with what is probably its powered companion attending to the port wing tanks. The seemingly pristine condition of the bomber suggests it has been directly assigned to No. 83 OTU at Peplow, Shropshire, as opposed to being relegated from previous operational duties.

The Wellington was a regular feature on support units such as the manifold OTUs scattered throughout the British mainland. Mk. X HE508 has landed at a USAAF airfield, judging by the nearby Jeep's insignia and the distinctive national uniform of the distant airman. The removal of the FN20 turret's central Plexiglas strip was a vital aid to visibility for the gunner when the bomber was conducting operations, prior to its transfer to a training status.

MK. X WELLINGTON SPECIFICATIONS

Wingspan	86 ft., 2 in.
Length	64 ft., 7 in.
Height	17 ft., 5 in.
All-up weight	36,000 lbs.
Powerplants	Hercules VI or XVI 1,675 hp radial engine

Armament

FN5 nose turret with two .303 machine guns
FN20 rear turret with four .303 machine guns
Two fuselage beam-mounted .303 machine guns

Performance

Max speed	255 mph
Service ceiling	22,000 ft.
Range	2,550 miles
Bombload	4,000 lbs.
Crew	5

The fabric covering to Mk. X MF244 has been largely stripped from the starboard stabilizer, while a similar effect applies to the rear fuselage undersides. The fact that the geodetic structure remains intact is a testament to its overall integrity. Note how the entire central Plexiglas panel is detached from the FN20 rear turret, thereby providing the gunner with added visibility.

Ops are on and the rapidly deteriorating late afternoon or evening sky still provides a visual background for a line of Wellingtons as they taxi out toward the selected runway end. The Vickers-Armstrong design was in the forefront of Bomber Command operations up to late 1942, prior to the full-scale advent of its four-engine contemporaries, and soldiered on until withdrawal during October 1943.

The nonflight clothing worn by this rear gunner is adequate for flying sorties with the SEAC theater. HZ550's FN20 turret demonstrates its greater dimensions compared to the FN10 twin-gun unit. The aircraft is believed to be serving with No. 99 Squadron, then based at Jessore, India. Note the "Monica" tail-warning aerial, which would tend to be redundant in the Far East thanks to the lack of Japanese night fighters.

No. 99 Squadron's association with the Wellington harks back to late 1938, with conversion onto the Mk. I. By 1944, the squadron was well entrenched in the Far East (India), with service at Digri and Jessore, where this view of personnel partially shaded by a Mk. X's engine nacelle was taken. The double-shaded blue roundel and fin flash on the other Wellington were standard markings in this theater of operations.

No. 466 Squadron, established in 1942, was one of the Australian-nominated units within Bomber Command. The initial Mk. III Wellington cadre was gradually replaced by the Mk. X, one of whose number has the port Hercules engine, with its distinctive broad-bladed propeller and spinner cover under full investigation. Operations are indicated by foaming pints of a favorite Scottish beer being quaffed by a full-bearded character.

If ever a picture content demonstrated the structural integrity of the Wellington, it is revealed here by Mk. X NA: Y/NA239. Flak over the target at Duisburg on March 8–9, 1943, excised the rear turret along with its hapless occupant. Despite this potentially mortal blow, the pilot was able to retain his charge aloft and land it back on a British airfield.

No. 426 (RCAF) Squadron received the Mk. X Wellington in March 1943; however, within three months the "Thunderbird" unit converted to the Mk. II Lancaster. The closely parked nature of the Wellington lineup is unconsciously indicative of the sense of overall invulnerability from enemy aircraft assault by this stage of World War II.

BJ780 was declared MIA off a minelaying operation on October 9, 1942. The No. 12 Squadron Mk. X is seen with a fractured fuselage and under enemy inspection. It is likely that the bomber was fatally crippled close to the coast, whereupon the pilot succeeded in avoiding crashing into the sea but could not prevent this heavy impact into a wooded area. There is a good chance that some, or all, of the crew survived the incident.

The second picture, shot from directly behind, shows how the elevator rod on the massively damaged rear airframe has thankfully been left intact, allowing control to be maintained.

HE575, unlike the majority of its Mk. X contemporaries, never saw active service; instead it was assigned from the Chester factory in early 1943 to the first of several training units. In this instance the Y7 codes denote service with No. 61 OTU at Gamston.

The Mk. X seen in this photograph bears a faired-in nose turret and a fuselage reversion to exposure for the original fuselage window Plexiglas. These seemingly retrograde steps conceal the fact that "Sister Anna," as the crew named her, has been switched from a bomber to a transport role in the Mediterranean theater. Sgt. Jack Wade (WOP/AG) stands second from the right.

This is a comprehensive view of "Sister Anna," which bore the serial LP201. The Wellington bears a color scheme that matches the one borne by its Coastal Command contemporaries, but not with the same hostile intention behind its deployment. The photo angle confirms the fairing-in of the rear turret and the limiting of markings to the aircraft letter "L."

The minuscule diameter of the main wheels depicted on Mk. X BK563 would indicate that their ability to function properly during landing and takeoff would be problematical compared to normal-size wheels. In fact, these Dunlop "Compacta" fittings that were also applied to Lancaster PB672, albeit in slightly larger format, proved to be sound in their performance but were never brought into RAF service following the 1946 experiment.

Two crew members on an anonymous Polish squadron Mk. X are gazing down upon a Tiger Moth, the RAF's primary trainer for pilots. A second Tiger Moth can be seen landing in the left background, suggesting that the bomber was photographed at a flying training school (FTS). The contrast in scale and structural strength between the duo of aircraft is evident.

"The Sea Shall Not Have Them" is the well-earned motto of the RAF Air/Sea Rescue service, whose personnel in this case have located the dinghy containing two of the crew from a No. 166 Squadron Mk. X. The duo of undoubtedly exhausted as well as relieved airmen was adrift for five days in their terribly exposed canvas vessel following the ditching of HE862/AS: L off a raid to Mannheim on April 16, 1943. A bar of chocolate, Horlicks tablets, and rainwater were their critically limited means of sustenance.

Gen. "Jimmy" Doolittle, CG of the Northwest African Air Force (NWAAF), *second from left*, prepares to board a No. 150 Squadron Mk. X on February 22, 1943. The former leader of the April 17, 1942, raid on Tokyo would undertake several operational flights during World War II, including this sortie against the docks at Bizerte, launched from Blida in Algeria. General-ranked personnel were not encouraged to do this, for fear of being shot down and captured to face the certain act of interrogation.

A second picture taken at the RAF airfield of Blida picks out a clutch of Allied aircraft types. A Boston stands in the right background, with a P-51A adjacent to the Douglas bomber's starboard wing. Four Hurricanes are buzzing the airfield following completion of a sortie; they are watched by a group of personnel standing around the nose of a Mk. X parked in front of a hangar.

The need for Coastal Command aircraft to remain invisible as much as possible to enemy surface vessels, and especially U-boats, witnessed the increasing substitution of overall camouflage with white. In this case the dark areas originally sprayed on No. 221 Squadron's DF: O/W5674 were reduced to a thin dorsal fuselage strip, along with retention on the upper wing surfaces. Photo taken at Reykjavik, Iceland.

The Battle of the Atlantic, being the main campaign that gave Winston Churchill the most sleepless nights and frightened him mightily, was arguably also the key to winning the European war. Every measure, whether on the sea or in the air, that could counter the U-boat threat had to be fully indulged, if that threat to the marine logistical life line, with the route from the United States central to Britain's survival, had not only to be countered but permanently nullified.

Airpower facilities were critical to the campaign's overall successful conduct but were sadly lacking in terms of numbers, suitability for duty, and, equally important, effective range during the initial years of the battle. Equally lacking were the requisite number of custom-built escorts equipped with electronic means that could detect the enemy predators. This latter technical deficiency applied both to surface and airborne forces but was being addressed by 1941. However, there arose a frustrating limitation in terms of night flights when applied to Coastal Command aircraft. The lower the aircraft flew, the quicker it was for back echoes off the surface to swallow up the reflective signals on the radar screen, denoting a possible target. In the case of such nocturnal sorties, a brilliant visual solution that was the brainchild of S/Ldr. Humphrey De Verde Leigh was based on a searchlight mounted on or within the aircraft.

The test platform for his innovative scheme was an operationally redundant DWI Wellington, into which a generator to supply the required power was inserted. The initial searchlight choice focused on an army 90 cm unit, but attention was quickly switched to a more compact and maneuverable 60 cm naval equivalent. The Wellington's redundant ventral turret hatch provided the convenient access for the light beam, with the equipment capable of being deployed and retracted through the aperture. The light's movement was controlled by the same Frazer Nash hydraulic gear that operated the FN gun turrets; its presence permitted an extremely precise focal facility both in elevation and azimuth.

All was proceeding in order with the equipment, but elsewhere an alternate scheme was being created by a G/Capt. Helmore. His device was based on Fighter Command's Bostons that had been adapted to carry a searchlight in the nose, with which to illuminate enemy bombers for an accompanying Hurricane to down. The key weakness with the arrangement lay with its positioning. The beam being in line with the cockpit critically affected the crew's visual acuity, unlike with the Leigh Light, which was positioned well below their sight line. The air officer commanding (AOC) of Coastal Command, A. M. Joubert de la Ferte, was sufficiently enamored of Helmore's project to order cancellation of the Leigh Light. What was clearly a major and crushing blow for S/Ldr. Leigh proved thankfully short lived. The AOC reviewed the situation (and subsequently admitted his haste in making the choice); S/Ldr. Leigh's system was resurrected, and the experiment proceeded.

The initial successful test occurred over the Irish Sea on May 4, 1941, with Leigh on board. The Royal Navy's submarine H-31 was illuminated, and afterward officers on the crew confirmed that the Wellington was not observed until the light beam was activated; the time span between this and the bomber's arrival over the warship granted no evasive measure to be successfully indulged.

Adaptation of a surprisingly small figure of fifty-eight Mk. ICs to the revised GR Mk. VIII was duly carried out. The relatively new ASV Mk. I radar set was also installed along with its external

A GR Mk. VIII is photographed flying at around 50 feet, the height at which the currently retracted Leigh Light beam would be exposed. The aircraft bears the early Coastal Command scheme of gray/green top colors over white sides and undersurfaces, and the code letters bear an unusual light-gray-and-red mix. Aircraft is believed to be with No. 172 Squadron, although the WM unit code cannot be absolutely confirmed as being so allotted.

BB466, based at Shandur in North Africa, was another Mk. 1C that was converted to a GR Mk. VIII status. In this instance the Wellington still bears the darker camouflage pattern applicable to aircraft operating with Bomber Command. Picture taken during 1942 reveals the aircraft in pristine condition, with the dorsal fuselage and starboard wing-mounted aerials in clear view. Aircraft was "ditched" on December 1 while serving with No. 221 Squadron.

aerial array on the fuselage's top and side surfaces, which were supplemented by large YAGI aerials under the outer wings. A key and necessary change was the detaching of the FN5 nose turret in favor of a Plexiglas frame akin to that carried by the Mk. I. The Leigh Light operator was the obvious beneficiary of the fitting.

Two units were destined to carry out operations with the equipment, beginning with No. 172 Squadron, based at Chivenor in southwestern England, a zone from where Coastal Command patrolled the Bay of Biscay. The aircraft range was expanded by the insertion of fuel cells into the outer bomb bay lengths, with six depth charges loaded into the central length. The nonstandard crew consisted of two pilots, a navigator, and three wireless operator / air gunners (WOPs), an abbreviation later and perhaps diplomatically altered to WAG (wireless operator / air gunner). The navigator was tasked with the Leigh Light's operation. He would activate the system but was additionally responsible for releasing the depth charges.

Up to now, the U-boat crews had been free from nocturnal interdiction as they traversed the bay on the surface; the twin benefit arising from this action was the ability to recharge the vessel's diesel batteries, apart from which a higher speed could be maintained compared to the submersible equivalent. This immunity from attack

was set to be badly compromised with the arrival of No. 172 Squadron's specialist Wellingtons. On June 4, 1942, the Italian submarine *Torelli* was caught squarely in the bomber's beam and, although depth-charged, managed to reach a port in a severely damaged condition. At this point, No. 179 Squadron was declared operational and joined in the action. Another important advance was the availability of radio altimeters. These guaranteed a better prospect of avoiding flying too low, as well as ensuring that the 50-foot attack altitude was accurately achieved; several "contacts" had been compromised due to the run-in height being miscalculated.

On July 5, P/O Howell, an American who had joined the RAF prior to Pearl Harbor, achieved the first confirmed kill by No. 172 Squadron, with U-502 and its crew the unfortunate casualty. This was the first of an admittedly small number of victories for the RAF. On the other hand, the effect on the Kriegsmarine personnel's morale was surely high and remained so until a flexible scanning aerial that was clipped to the conning tower when surfaced and was known as Das Biscayankreuz (Biscay Cross) made its appearance during 1942–43. The Metox set that the aerial was linked with could pick up ASV signals from as far away as 30 miles, a measure that had a notable impact on the Wellington crews' ability to spring a surprise on their nautical adversaries.

GR Mk. VIII Torpedo Bomber

An appreciably large batch of Mk. IC Wellingtons, 175 in all, were adapted to a torpedo-bomber role under the same GR Mk. VIII nomenclature. They bore the ASV MK. II gear and the same external array of "Stick" and Yagi aerials as their Leigh Light contemporaries, but the operational theater for most, if not all, the aircraft concerned was in the Mediterranean. Malta's central location within the sea, which also lay astride the Axis convoy routes from southern Europe, made it an ideal location for shipping strikes. Although ever open to interception by fighters, especially the longer-range Bf 110 and even the Ju 88C, the RAF crews succeeded in playing a crucial part in the battle to deprive the Afrikakorps and its Italian counterpart of the means to sustain their North African campaign. This was especially important during the several months surrounding the Battle of El Alamein, which finally broke the enemy's resistance and propelled its forces inexorably toward final defeat eight months later.

The trolley being pushed forward by an airman bears what looks like two depth charges (*left*) along with a pair of bombs. The aircraft's light overall color and what appears to be Pegasus engines indicate it is a GR VIII torpedo bomber, given the absence of the ASV Mk. II external aerials borne by the Leigh Light equivalent.

A torpedo-bomber version of the GR Mk. VIII bears the same external outline as the Leigh Light Wellington, with two distinct differences. The clean ventral line of the rear fuselage does not reveal the Leigh Light's bulge when retracted, while the nose turret is faired over compared to the normal Plexiglas frame for the Leigh Light operator's use; however, the latter modification was not always applied.

The lead Wellington from this duo of GR Mk. VIII has just released its torpedo during a practice exercise. The aircraft's height at this point was a critical factor in ensuring the weapon entered the sea at the correct angle; otherwise it was not guaranteed to follow the correct track. The necessarily steady flight path rendered the bomber open to potentially deadly focus by a convoy's gunners.

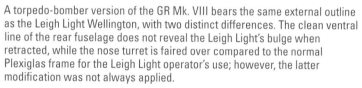

A Wellington torpedo bomber forms the backdrop to one of the antishipping weapons mounted on its trolley and ready for installation in the aircraft's bomb bay. The slim lines of the torpedo are evident, and the need to amend the bomb bay with its longitudinal beams would appear to be minimal.

CHAPTER 11
GR Mks. XI to XIV

The GR Mk. XI Wellington—"GR," standing for general reconnaissance—was the first of four Hercules-powered variants to serve in a maritime role with Coastal Command. HZ258 displays the basic lighter camouflage pattern used by the command to conceal the aircraft from enemy observation, although the brown/green upper colors would soon give way to a gray/green variation. This No. 304 (Polish) Squadron aircraft lacks the ASV aerials for the Mk. II radar sets with which to track down U-boats or surface vessels.

The original decision to develop a torpedo-bomber version of the Wellington commenced with a 271-strong batch of Mk. IC airframes in 1940–41. Most of these aircraft had devolved to North Africa, where they interdicted the Axis convoy routes coming south from Italy. Their existence along with the Leigh Light Wellingtons encouraged the RAF to coordinate planning with Vickers for more custom-built airframes that would serve Coastal Command in comprehensive antisubmarine as well as antishipping operations. (Although important, the former target category represented a measurably greater threat to the Allied cause's advance and likely gained a priority in application compared to shipping strikes.)

In time, the first of four subvariants, all under the prefix General Reconnaissance (GR) and Mk. X in basic layout, were duly produced and joined the maritime command, the batch of 180 being split between Weybridge (105) and Blackpool (75). The GR Mk. XI was intended as a torpedo bomber as well as bearing the ASV Mk. II radar equipment. The presence of the same external aerial masts and stubs as the GR Mk. VIII clearly marked those aircraft so outfitted; the percentage of airframes not so altered could be ascribed to the batch only by their serials, however.

The practice of spraying Coastal Command aircraft in low-visibility colors of gray over white was perhaps surprisingly absent on these Wellingtons, which retained the Bomber Command scheme. On the other hand, the stalking and low-level-attack approach would probably be effective regardless of color patterns, up to the point where the target run-in commenced. From then on, the presence of flak ships and weapons on the convoy vessels would turn the assault into a survival lottery, given the steady pace and bulk of the aircraft, especially during daylight operations; nocturnal operations would appear to provide an enhanced chance of clearing a convoy successfully.

The GR Mk. XII represented the first of two variants to bear the aerodynamically clean ASV Mk. III radar in a comprehensive manner, although some GR Mk. XIs had reportedly been similarly accoutered. The 10-centimeter-wavelength signal emitted by the magnetron valve, which was the key centerpiece of the equipment, allowed for the removal of all but the most minuscule external aerials, which furthermore provided a far more precise directional scan to pick out targets with. The set was now housed in a lower nose-mounted teardrop fairing, with an upper-nose Plexiglas turret frame reminiscent of that borne by the Mk. I.

There was no custom-built armament installed, but recourse was soon had to mounting two .303 machine guns. The practice at the time for any U-boats surprised while on the surface was for the crews to bring their formidable range of gunfire to bear on an attacking aircraft rather than seek salvation by diving. The steady approach by any Coastal Command aircraft of the Wellington's dimension left it vulnerable to heavy if not fatal damage; the nose-positioned weaponry, although no more than adequate in striking power, at least served to hinder the Kriegsmarine sailors in their defensive task.

The relatively small batch of fifty-eight aircraft plied their trade over the near Atlantic, with the Bay of Biscay a regular area under surveillance since the zone was the initial departure and ultimate return stages of U-boat patrols. Given the imbalance in offensive to defensive firepower, aircraft losses inevitably occurred during a one-to-one encounter with an enemy vessel. Consequently, a change in operational policy witnessed any crew sighting a marine adversary to adopt a shadowing role, calling up reinforcements, and only then joining in on the multifold assault.

A real and virtually unchallengeable threat to U-boats arose with the arrival of the homing torpedo, which was given the cover title of "Mk. 24 Mine." Once normally launched at the point where the U-boat had already submerged—this being a measure intended to conceal the weapon's existence from any eyewitness—the result was almost always respective destruction and death for the vessel and its crew. The relatively small disturbance the explosion caused in the sea depths was a visually disappointing sight for the airmen, and confirmation usually arrived from subsequent monitoring of the German radio and similar transmissions.

The return to ASV Mk. II–equipped Wellingtons involved the GR Mk. XIII, of which no fewer than 842 were produced, some of which retained the Bomber Command camouflage pattern. Engine power was provided by the Hercules XVII, whose rating of 1,735 hp

was the greatest output provided by the Bristol-produced engine. The operational function of the variant was the same as its Mk. XI predecessor—namely, antishipping sorties—and these were conducted both in the northern European and Mediterranean theaters.

The quartet of GR-prefixed, Hercules-powered Wellingtons was completed by the Mk. XIV, which in concert with the GR Mk. XII was equipped with the ASV Mk. III radar equipment as well as the Leigh Light. Production numbers were virtually equal to the GR Mk. XIII, but with all three production plants involved in the figure of 841. Lack of forward firing armament would seem to be a retrograde measure on daylight operations. However, by the 1943–44 period of World War II, aerial superiority, if not total, was witnessing the drawing of the aerial string around the neck of the Luftwaffe's countereffort, which by D-day was totally overwhelmed in the skies over France.

The Wellingtons were to prove part of the bid to deny the Kriegsmarine U-boat fleet any access to the massive flow of shipborne materials wending their way across the English Channel to Normandy. Their planned interdiction of the shipping lanes was rendered totally moribund, with ten U-boats definitely sunk, one of which fell victim to a Wellington from No. 304 (Polish) Squadron; doubtless, its contemporaries were diverted from their nefarious intention by the presence of a Wellington hovering within the target zone.

What is probably a GR Mk. XI, to judge by the absence of an ASV scanner under the nose, has its Hercules engine revved up to full pitch as it prepares to depart from its dispersal. The red/white quartered emblem on the nose confirms this is a Polish-staffed unit, although which Coastal Command squadron is unknown. Adding to the confusion between the Mk. XI and XIII is that not all in the former category bore the ASV Mk. II external aerial array.

A GR Mk. XII has completed its operational service and is now seen after being ignominiously dumped into an area more resembling a pasture than an airfield. It lies in the company of what is a Bomber Command–assigned "Wimpy." The reason for application of the "X" letters is not known.

World War II had been over for fully two years when this picture of a GR Mk. XIII was taken. The Wellington bears its full array of ASV Mk. II aerials despite currently serving with the Empire Air Navigation School (AENS), based at Lindholme, Yorkshire; it is also still clad in the original Coastal Command color scheme.

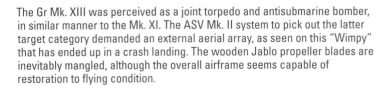

The Gr Mk. XIII was perceived as a joint torpedo and antisubmarine bomber, in similar manner to the Mk. XI. The ASV Mk. II system to pick out the latter target category demanded an external aerial array, as seen on this "Wimpy" that has ended up in a crash landing. The wooden Jablo propeller blades are inevitably mangled, although the overall airframe seems capable of restoration to flying condition.

Following the end of World War II, the French navy (Aeronaval) took on several GR Mk. XIIIs, MO771 being one. The ASV MK. II aerial array was retained by the French, whose reverse-color fin flash and roundels, along with an anchor imposed upon the latter marking, are on view in this picture. The top surface camouflage appears to have been removed in favor of an overall white scheme.

A line of Wellingtons occupy part of the Brooklands Aviation repair center based at Sywell, Nottinghamshire. Nearest to the camera is Mk. XIII ME898, bearing the full aerial array for an ASV Mk. II set. Despite the external display, the aircraft currently serves with No. 6 (C) OTU. The picture likely was taken in the final months of World War II, judging by what appears to be a type C fuselage roundel.

The Polish air force was involved with all RAF commands, including Coastal Command. The airfield is St. Eval in southwestern England, and a GR Mk. XIV serving with No. 304 (Polish) Squadron is taxiing past several fellow-squadron Wellingtons. Being located on the channel coast, the QO-coded aircraft were involved in successfully blocking the passage of U-boats attempting to interfere with the Normandy landings at this June 1944 period.

Chivenor in southwestern England forms the April 1944 scene for a GR Mk. XIV serving with No. 612 (County of Aberdeen) Squadron, one of twenty-five Royal Auxiliary Air Force (RAAF) units. A further three Mk. XIV–equipped squadrons are currently operating from the airfield in a bid to track down U-boats. The WAAF driver is Leading Aircraftswoman (LACW) Felicity Lambert.

The positioning as well as the extent of the fabric surface's absence on the inner wing area presents somewhat of a puzzle. The intact geodetic frame apparently rules out gunfire effect, whether aircraft or flak-delivered, while the nonscorched surround rules out fire. The color scheme on HF330/2N is the standard low-visibility scheme favored by Coastal Command.

The Rock of Gibraltar is a salient geographic feature in this picture, with the main airfield sheltering in its massive shadow. What is quoted as a GR Mk. XIV assigned to No. 458 (RAAF) Squadron is taking off, with a second example squatting in a partially exposed manner in the foreground. The outline of both the Mk. XII and XIV was similar, so the only clue to a variant's status relates to its serial, which is absent here.

No. 38 Squadron's association with the "Wimpy" commenced in late 1938, when it served within Bomber Command. Transfer to North Africa during 1942 and then onto Coastal Command duties in April 1943 followed. Mk. XIV NB895/G is in the company of another squadron aircraft on what is probably an antishipping sortie, this being the unit's primary task. The fuselage roundel's color dimensions indicate a late World War II period.

The Azores Islands, belonging to neutral Portugal, became the location for Allied airfields in late 1943, and Nos. 172 and 179 Squadrons deployed detachments there. The no. 1 applied to a GR Mk. XIV's rear fuselage denotes No. 172, but the return to full squadron codes was later made. The aircraft are operating from Lagens on Terceira, whose rugged landscape is captured in the picture.

There is some mystery as to this GR Wellington's lineage. The nose configuration indicates the aircraft is either a Mk. XII or XIV, both variants having the normal nose turret detached in favor of the Plexiglas frame. However, the ASV Mk. III set, enclosed within a lower nose fairing, is not on hand. Note the unusual camouflage separation line that was usually raised to the fuselage top edge on the GR Mk. XI/XIV series.

CHAPTER 12
C Mk. XV and XVI

An original Mk. 1A N2990 switched to transport duty now bears the markings for No. 24 Squadron and is photographed during 1943 at Hendon in North London, now the site for the RAF Museum. The camouflage pattern is believed to be Dark Earth / Dark Green over gray undersides, and the aircraft bears the title "Duke of Cornwall"; the specific reason for the title remains unknown to the author.

The lack of custom-built transport aircraft with which to back up the comprehensive transit of personnel and equipment dogged the RAF during the bulk of World War II. Apart from American-built sources, the accent was largely based on a make-and-mend basis, with the Wellington one of the designs entering the technical equation, albeit on a retrospective basis. The withdrawal of the earlier Marks from operational service provided the grounds for IA and IC airframes to be suitably adapted, but the precise details of internal adjustment remain unclear. The C Mk. IA, subsequently retitled the C Mk. XV, possessed fairings in place of the gun turrets and the insertion of a door into the central starboard fuselage. The absence of defensive firepower was visually countered on some aircraft by the painting of frame lines on the fuselage fairing to present the impression of gun mountings; fortunately, by the aircrafts' arrival on the operational scene, the *Jagdwaffe*'s influence on Allied aircraft traffic was steadily and inexorably waning.

Its Mk. IC companion bore a similar original title (C Mk. IC), but it was similarly changed to C Mk. XVI. This time around, there was no pretense at defensive firepower on hand. Instead, nose and tail cones replaced the turrets, so providing the sole external difference with its C Mk. XV "twin." There is no confirmation of how many airframes were involved in the project, but the concerned aircraft provided a solid service, especially after the Allied air forces' fighter and medium-bomber squadrons decamped to the Continent in 1944–45; the other operational theaters were not forgotten either.

A companion No. 24 Squadron C Mk. XV to the foregoing Wellington is similarly granted a "dukedom" title, in this instance for the county of Rutland. This airframe has been more civilianized in that the turret locations have given way to conical fairings. The fuselage window strip has also been farther extended to a point just ahead of the roundel.

A Mk. 1C converted to C Mk. XVI function displays its faired-over turrets, which do not retain any false frame lines as seen on C Mk. XV N2990. Although now a passenger transport, N2875 is assigned to the Central Gunnery School at Catfoss. Diamond-pattern shapes directly behind the small fuselage door are believed to be first-aid kits sown into the fabric.

CHAPTER 13

T Mk. XVII/XVIII / Mk. XIX

The serial number cannot be discerned on this Wellington variant, but official records state it is a Mk. XVIII. The bulbous nose reportedly houses an SCR720 radar set that is American in origin. The purpose of the Mk. XVIII was to train navigators and wireless operators, in the first case doubtless for operations on night fighters. Picture was taken in November 1944.

The introduction of antishipping radar within Coastal Command soon led to the need to instruct the aircrew tasked with the equipment's operation. Conversion of selected GR Mk. XI Wellingtons under the title T Mk. VII, which were in effect airborne radar classrooms, provided the necessary means. The T Mk. XIX was a service conversion of the Mk. X that was reportedly utilized for the specific training of Wellington crews—a seeming anomaly, given the availability of hundreds of Wellingtons serving at any of the twenty-five OTUs on regular hand. In between came the T Mk. XVIII, eighty Mk. Xs forming the initial wartime cadre for an extended number of the variant, which would provide a similar service in training navigators and wireless operators (the latter redesignated air signalers) between 1945 and 1953. The T Mk. XVIII was structurally altered to accommodate nose-mounted radar in similar fashion to the T Mk. XVII—unlike the postwar T Mk. X airframes, which were not so altered and either retained their nose turrets or had the turrets replaced by fairings.

A more lateral view of a second Mk. XVIII RF413 that has been turned out in a silver finish confirms the fairing-over of the rear turret mounting. Also, on view is the small diamond-pattern Plexiglas frame directly ahead of the type A roundel. Note the propellers, which lack the normal spinner cover. A total of eighty Mk. X airframes were structurally converted in this manner, along with inclusion of the appropriate technical equipment.

CHAPTER 14
T MK. X

No. 5 Air Navigation School (ANS) was based at Lindholme, Yorkshire, and this picture of T Mk. 10 LP597 was taken during a 1947 public display, perhaps related to the annual celebration of the Battle of Britain. The aircraft is liberally festooned with whip aerials and bears a silver finish broken solely by the yellow fuselage band.

The end of World War II did not witness the disappearance of the Wellington from RAF ranks, and indeed the aircraft would soldier on for a further eight years, albeit in a passive role. The perceived need to train up navigators and air signalers (the latter an updated replacement for the wireless operator) witnessed a sizable number of Mk. Xs being switched from their role as a bomber to this duty. The involved aircraft were in most cases sprayed in a silver finish and had their interiors fitted out with the necessary technical equipment. The gun turrets were sometimes retained, albeit in an unarmed condition, but in many instances were detached and fairings substituted. Three air navigation schools (ANS)—Nos. 1, 5, and 6—and No. 201 Advanced Flying School (AFS) were created

and staffed with the Mk. X. An external indication of the aircrafts' training status was the application of a broad yellow band to the rear fuselage, as well as the various whip aerials adorning the fuselage top. In addition, the original extended fuselage window strips were stripped of their fabric covering. It was only during 1953 that the T Mk. X was withdrawn in favor of the more custom-adapted Vickers Valetta, and later the company's Varsity would occur.

Several aircraft served as engine test beds. LN175 was initially fitted out with the four-bladed propeller design, subsequently applied to the postwar Vickers Viking civil airliner, before progressing to evaluation of the Rolls-Royce Dart turboprop, intended for the four-engine Vickers Viscount airliner.

NG425 is a T Mk. 10 companion to LP597, but unlike the latter, it does not sport a succession of whip aerials on its dorsal surface. This feature indicates it is serving in the role of a prenavigation trainer. The film's autochromatic reaction has rendered the yellow color band in a seemingly black condition. Reversion to the original full fuselage window length was seen on many of this final operational Wellington variant.

The deletion of camouflage from the T Mk. 10 airframes occurred only once World War II was over, so early aircraft remained in their original state. The fuselage on this example bears a yellow rectangle as a visual backdrop to the roundel and unit code letters. This picture is believed to have been taken at Topcliffe, then home for No. 1 ANS.

The Wellington's distinctive low-slung fuselage that hugs the ground is well evident with T Mk. X NG892. Both the engines and the FN20 rear turret are liberally swathed in canvas covers with which to ward off the worst effects of the mercurial British weather conditions.

Several Mk. X Wellingtons were adapted as engine test beds during the late 1940s. This example is LN176, whose Hercules engines have been displaced by Rolls-Royce Dart turbines. The slim nature of the future power plant that will be installed in the Vickers Viscount is evident in the hangar close-up view.

LN176 is caught at the point of takeoff for another test flight in the series. Although involved in what is a civil engineering project, the aircraft is still an RAF aircraft, as signified by the fuselage and wing roundel markings and serial.

The sole complete Wellington airframe still in existence is MF628. It was originally finished in silver during its service as a T Mk. 10; however, it was subsequently sprayed in late World War II Bomber Command camouflage and markings and now is a permanent exhibit at the RAF Museum, Hendon, in North London.

CHAPTER 15
Warwick

The origins of the Vickers Warwick that relate to its predecessor are clearly outlined in this view of HF244 in flight. The fuselage extension and insertion of a FN50 middle-upper turret cannot conceal the design's genealogy. Delays in production, primarily due to a lack of efficient power, saw it enter service in 1943. The lifeboat slung underneath the ASR Mk. I, powered by the American Double Wasp, confirms this example's assignment to Coastal Command, with the D-day stripes confirming a mid-1944 operational period.

The immediate successor to the Wellington, named the Warwick, was the result of a response to specification B.1/35. The fuselage length of 96 ft., 81½ in. was 10 ft., 6 in. longer than the Wellington; the wingspan, varying between 72 ft., 3 in. (Mk. I) and 72 ft., 6 in. (Mk. V), exceeded the Wellington's standard 64 ft., 7 in. by a marginally smaller degree. The prototype (K8178) took to the air in August 1939, but as with the Avro Manchester, the choice of the in-line Rolls-Royce Vulture proved a major factor in the aircraft's disappointing performance. Unlike the Avro bomber, whose ultimate failure was due to official persistence with the inefficient Rolls-Royce engine, Vickers made a power switch to the Bristol Centaurus on L9704, and the result was a noticeable overall advance.

Any prospect for the aircraft assuming a role as a bomber was to remain dormant. The order for 250 aircraft placed in January 1941 was not initiated until July 1942. By this stage of the bombing offensive, the increasing availability of the Stirling, Halifax, and Lancaster on the operational scene was witnessing the days of twin-engine designs' participation becoming steadily redundant. A side problem was the shortage of supply vis-à-vis the Centaurus engine, whereupon the company adopted the option of the Pratt & Whitney Double Wasp, with a 1,850 hp rating, for the Mk. I. The aircraft was now allocated to Coastal Command in an air-sea rescue role. Nose, beam, and tail armament provision was the same as for the Mk. III Wellington, but with the addition of a FN50 dorsal turret; the latter unit would be deleted on the Mks. II and V, however.

Its lengthy fuselage proved a good platform for the carriage of the specialist Lindholme lifeboat, which was parachute-assisted upon release. No. 280 Squadron, at Langham in Norfolk, took on their first Mk. Is out of a final total of 275 airframes produced,

but a figure reduced by sixteen; the aircraft concerned were the first group turned out on the production line but never converted to the ASR function. The Mk. I achieved a maximum speed of 224 mph, a range of 2,300 miles, and a ceiling of 21,500 feet.; the loaded weight was 45,000 pounds. A total of fifteen squadrons were equipped with the Mk. I, of which six served in the Middle or Far East theaters.

The continuing availability of the Centaurus would power the second of the final total of three Warwick variants functioning in an active role during World War II. The Mk. II was allocated a general reconnaissance role, with 133 aircraft so outfitted. Finally, there arrived the Mk. V, which bore the Centaurus, which was rated at 2,250 hp and was produced to the tune of 210. A noticeable external alteration was the removal of the nose turret in favor of a bay window frame. A radar scanner was mounted under the forward nose area, and a Leigh Light was installed behind the bomb bay, the intention being for the aircraft to serve as an antisubmarine aircraft. However, its operational service was limited to No. 179 Squadron, stationed in southwestern England; the Japanese surrender preempted any intention to deploy the Mk. V to the Far East. Postwar service was to prove brief, with Lancasters assuming the duty. Fourteen Mk. Vs were detached to act as meteorological aircraft with No. 520 Squadron, based at Gibraltar.

HF547 is another Mk. I Warwick that in its case is apparently serving in the Far East, the SNAKE lettering below the serial acting as confirmation. The forward-angle view shows up the shape of the Pratt & Whitney Double Wasp, which was an emergency measure due to a shortage in supplies of the planned Bristol Centaurus. A French Ju 52 appears in the right background.

HG238 is one of a hundred airframes converted to a transport function under the Mk. III nomenclature, with the adaptation of an extended "pannier" structure located over the length of the bomb bay. This is another Warwick bearing the SNAKE indication for Far East service, although records suggest the design never progressed beyond the Middle East in terms of unit assignment. Note the shape of the rear entrance door and the faired-over rear turret mount.

A second view of HG238 shows how a second modification to the nose area sees the FN5 turret replaced by a slimmer cone shape incorporating an oval Plexiglas frame at its base. The SEAC double-blue roundels visible on the aircraft in the previous picture add to the puzzle as to whether the Warwick ever advanced to the Far East, where the marking was a salient feature.

In addition to the three actively operated Marks came two of a passive nature, although the first was adapted out of Mk. I stock. The RAF was woefully lacking in custom-built transport aircraft, with nothing on the scale of the USAAF's C-47, C-46, and C-54 other than the Avro York, based on the Lancaster. In Vickers' case, fourteen Mk. Is were modified, with the insertion of nose and tail cones in place of the gun turrets. Their function was limited to the movement of supplies of mail to the Middle East theater, and they were flown by British Overseas Airways Corporation (BOAC) crews.

Not only was the subsequent Mk. III transport built as a specific batch of one hundred, but the interiors were fitted out for the carriage of between eight to ten senior military personnel or twenty-four officers or other ranks. The freight-loading aspect was not forgotten and, in the Mk. III's case, was accomplished by the attachment of a pannier extending along the bomb bay length and protruding below the line of the ventral fuselage, and capable of bearing loads up to 6,710 pounds. Four squadrons in Nos. 46 and 47 Groups of Transport Command were assigned the variant between August 1944 and the summer of 1945. No. 301 converted onto the Halifax VIII, which bore the same pannier-based outline during January 1946, and by May the Warwick had been removed from the remaining three squadrons' establishment of aircraft.

The GR Mk. V, of which 210 airframes were constructed, was the final variant of the Warwick to emerge. Engine power by the time of its emergence was the planned Bristol Centaurus. The location for the Leigh Light and nose-mounted radar scanner, which were utilized for antisubmarine operations, is visible. The Warwick was displaced by ASR Mk. III Lancasters during 1946.

No. 179 Squadron, based at St. Eval in southwestern England, was the first Coastal Command unit to take on the GR Mk. V, in November 1944. The low-level nature of operations against submarines was usually conducted at night and could be the reason for the deletion of the middle-upper FN50 turret, as displayed by the Warwick in the background. The bay window Plexiglas replacement for the Mk. I's and II's nose turret was a distinctive feature of the variant.

In 1985, the remains of Mk. IA N2980 were hauled out of Loch Ness. On December 31, 1940, the bomber, now serving with No. 20 OTU following active operations with Nos. 149 and 37 Squadrons, had been "ditched" due to power loss. The picture shows the aircraft undergoing the transformation into its original condition during the 1990s. Since then, the wings—complete with Pegasus engines—have been similarly restored, leaving the aircraft the sole other Wellington airframe in current existence, albeit not yet as externally finished as the RAF Museum's T Mk. 10.